WORDBRIDGE

WORDBRIDGE

A Collection
Of
Lyrical Poems

Edward Pizzella

To order additional copies of this book, contact:
Xlibris
1-888-795-4274
www.Xlibris.com
Orders@Xlibris.com
712723

CONTENTS

Dedication...xi
Author's Bio..xiii
Acknowledgements...xvii

Aaron's Song..236
Actors All..31
Adam's Rib...4
Alyssa's Toad..43
Amending The Gender Of God 2
America's Mayor..12
Amor Est...181
Anatomy Of A Boycott..211
Ant And The Grasshopper, The 122
Ars Gratia Artis 13
Artistic Differences..216
Autumn Leaves..138
Balloon Man, The..17
Beamer's Battle Cry..14
Beauty's Why And Wherefore..194
Belated Blame..221
Best Laid Plans, The 45
Beware The I'ds Of March..86
Bitten By The Bug..272
Blue As The Pleon..54
Calpurnia's Dream 23
Canine Design 139
Canine Mendacity 7
Captain On The Bridge, The 274
Cat At Mystic Cove, The...64
Cat-Atude 219

Celebrity 191
Chairs 140
Common Stuff 46
Consider The Lilies 47
Critic, The.. 115
Curious Conflagration 68
David's Debut... 147
Dimpled Chad Chicanery................................222
Discourse Of The Muse, The............................91
Doublespeak...96
Electoral Depression 223
Elusive Love 49
Era Of The Duck, The 50
Essence Of Diplomacy, The 53
Eternal City.. 213
Etymology 10
Expressions Of Love 238
Eye Of A Needle, The 20
Fallen Hero.. 105
Fiction Of Addiction, The 239
Flaw And Order 134
Flight Of The Bumblebee, The 149
Fox And The Crow, The................................... 119
Freckles 218
Functions Of The Heart, The 151
Gender Yap 120
God's Precious Gem 78
Happiness For Hire.. 15
Haven On The Lake 56
His Empty Shoes 57
House On Quinte Isle, The 107
Identity Crisis, The 63
If There's A Stage... 156
I Love A Parade 59
Impressions Of My Lady...................................30
Inspired By The Mews 220
Ironically Irish 89
I Stopped To Say Hello....................................256

Knight To Remember, A 102
Lawyer's Lament, A 60
Legacy Of Luck...94
Legal Aspects.. 16
Legal Opinion, A 66
Lemon's Bitter Pill 87
Lesson, The 28
Lest Ye Be Judged 112
Life's Alias 83
Life's Ill-Design 77
Light At Peggy's Cove, The 110
Lily's Song 229
Little White Lies 262
Love Of A Rainy Day 240
Love's Harvest..242
Marriage Debate, The 245
Martyrs? 210
Message Of His Life, The...252
Metamorphoses Of Spring 109
Mirror Of Love..247
Moose On The Loose..253
Mother Of Spills, The 259
My Favorite Plumber 231
My Laptop 224
My Second Born 233
Nautical Paradox, A 19
Nightmare, The 62
Nine-One-One 85
Nocturnal Treasures 176
Nonni's Loving Hands.. 145
Northend Review 248
Ode To A Four-Letter Word..208
Ode To An Ugly Lamp 164
Ode To Wayward Socks..80
Old Glory's Dimensions 243
Owed To A Persistent Creditor....................................... 182
Paradox Of Love, The 246
Pathology 207

Pause That Refreshes, The..178
Perspective...82
Pesky Demons..254
Phoenix And The Feline..204
Picking Out A Beau..192
Pinball Machine, The...36
P. J. Topcat...270
Poet's Will, A...184
Portrait Of Love, A...170
Power Of A Eulogy, The...39
Practice Of The Dove, The..41
Price Of Survival, The...260
Prince Of Isles, The...123
Professional Pride...133
Prolific Pixels..228
Prologue To Eternity...206
Pursuit Of Happiness, The..179
Quest For Asylum..264
Rendering, The..61
Reparations..266
Requiem For A Poet...189
Rock Harbor Sunset..168
Round Pond Revisited...197
Rule Of De Minimus, The..137
Saga Of Kimberley Road, The..267
Sea Sense..193
Secret Of Life, The..188
Seduced By Sedona...117
Sexual Semantics..175
Significance Of Saucers, The...72
Simplicity...185
Sleeping Beauty...34
Sonnet Of Sanity...6
Sound Of The Written Word, The...190
Sour Grapes...125
Supping Seagulls...186
Surgical Alternative, A..9
Surrender?...203

Temptation's Call..202
Tempus Fugit 173
That's Cats...127
Thousand Words, A 227
Timely Theme, A..180
To Love Another 76
Too Late To Say Goodbye..93
Tribute To San Antonio, A..131
Ultimate Wager, The 187
Undercover...70
Virtue Of Hypocrisy, The 258
Visit With Friends, A 195
Vital Vittles 159
Vive La Difference..177
What Government Gives..22
What's My Line? 257
Wisdom In Reflection...84
Wordbridge..1
Word Power..129
Words Of Love..114

DEDICATION

This work is dedicated to my teachers at Northeast Junior High School and Weaver High School in Hartford, Connecticut, and, in particular, to my Guidance Councilor, Benjamin O'Connell, and my eighth grade English teacher, Miss Hoye. They instilled in me a burning desire to learn and, along with my loving parents, were my primary inspiration and motivation for academic achievement. Miss Hoye introduced me to poetry, not two dimensional poetry or poetry on the written page, but three dimensional poetry, the beautifully penetrating sound of poetic expression. She would require her students to memorize classical poems and then recite them with passion before the class. I threw myself whole-heartedly into this exercise and grew to love not only the language, but the sound of the language.

Northeast Junior High School annually held an oratorical contest and Mr. O'Connell encouraged me to participate. My experiences with poetic recitation in English class provided me with the confidence I needed. I won the contest and was designated a speaker at graduation.

The local Civitan Club annually presented an award to the junior high student with the best citizenship and scholastic record. With his recommendation I was granted this Award. I attribute much of my academic and professional success to the inspiration I received from these devoted mentors.

AUTHOR'S BIO

 Ed Pizzella is a lawyer, politician, consumer advocate, actor, director, producer, writer and, last but not least, a poet. A child of the Great Depression, Mr. Pizzella is the offspring of Italian immigrants. Born in the Italian ghetto of Hartford, Connecticut, he attended local public schools, where, by his heritage, he was driven to learn. Because he was born only a year after his mother arrived in this country, in his early years he spoke only Italian. He soon mastered English and at Northeast Junior High School in Hartford was elected to the National Honor Society, won the school's oratorical contest and was a graduation speaker and a recipient of the Civitan Award.

His appreciation of poetry commenced in his eighth grade English class, where he studied the classics and excelled in recitation. He was attracted to languages and avidly studied Latin, French and Italian. He also acquired a profound interest in mythology.

At Weaver High School in Hartford he wrote for the school newspaper, served as president of the French Club, was awarded the chemistry prize at graduation and ranked in the upper ten percent of his class. At Trinity College (Hartford) he majored in Romance Languages and in 1954 was graduated cum laude with a Bachelor of Arts degree. He received his Juris Doctor degree from the University of Connecticut School of Law in 1957, where he was graduated third in his class. He was admitted to the Connecticut Bar in 1957 and since that time has been actively engaged in the general practice of law.

While in law school, as a member of the Board of Student Editors (Law Review), he authored three articles which were published in the Connecticut Bar Journal. The last of the three, entitled "A Survey Of Connecticut Zoning Law," was subsequently republished in pamphlet form.

He was admitted to the Connecticut Bar in 1957 and is a member of the Connecticut Bar Association, the Federal District Court Bar for the District of Connecticut, the Second Circuit Court of Appeals Bar and the U. S. Supreme Court Bar.

He commenced legal practice as assistant legal aid attorney for the Legal Aid Society of Hartford County and, after he left that position to enter private practice, founded and chaired the Legal Aid Board of New Britain. He continued to hone his writing skills in the form of brief writing in the course of his extensive appellate practice. Writing became prominent in his civic and political activities, where, as President of the local Chamber of Commerce and as a local elected official, he penned numerous articles which were published in local newspapers.

He served as a member of the Newington Zoning Commission and as Chairman of the Zoning Board of Appeals. Upon his re-election, as a member of the Newington Town Council, received the highest number of votes. He also served as counsel for the Senate majority in the 1973 and 1974 state legislative sessions and in 1974, as counsel for the legislature's Banks and Regulated Activities Committee. In 1975 he was nominated as Newington's Republican candidate for Mayor and in 1995 as the Republican candidate for Probate Judge for the Newington Probate District.

In the late 1960's, Mr. Pizzella became active in community theatre and subsequently appeared in major roles in more than a hundred dinner theatre and community theatre productions in central Connecticut. He directed a number of theatrical productions for Theatre Newington and the Downstairs Cabaret in Newington, Connecticut, The OnStage Performers in Wolcott, Connecticut, L'Auberge d'Elegance Dinner Theatre in Bristol, Connecticut, Beckley

Dinner Theatre and The Connecticut Cabaret in Berlin, Connecticut, The Ramada Dinner Theatre in New Britain, Connecticut, and The Centre Stage Dinner Theatre in Meriden, Connecticut.

As one of the founders of Theatre One Productions, Inc., he assisted in producing nineteen major shows. He served as Business Manager for Theatre Newington, Secretary of Theatre One Productions, Chairman of the Tri-Town Community Cable Access Committee, Chairman of the Cox Cable Advisory Council and Vice-Chairman of the SNET State-wide Cable Advisory Council. He was a founder and served as Secretary of Newington Community Television, Inc., a local community access telecaster. He authored three theatrical reviews which were published in area newspapers. Many of his poems have been published in newspapers, on the internet and in anthologies.

Mr. Pizzella previously published a collection of poetry based upon Biblical passages entitled "Thy Will Be Done," which can be obtained from Amazon.com, and a memoir based upon his thirty-six years of theatrical experience entitled "The Versatility Of Chairs," which can be obtained from Xlibris Publishing Co.

ACKNOWLEDGEMENTS

"Sonnet Of Sanity" was published in the July 7, 1989 issue of the Newington Town Crier, a local newspaper; "Life's Ill-Design" appears in "A Delicate Balance," an anthology published by the National Library of Poetry; "Undercover," "Too Late To Say Goodbye" and "The Nightmare" appear in "Nature's Echoes," an anthology published by the International Library of Poetry; "Undercover" also appears in that publisher's anthology entitled "Poetry's Elite: The Best Poets of 2000;" "Surrender?" appears in "The Best Poems And Poets Of 2001," an anthology published by the International Library of Poetry; "The Essence Of Diplomacy" and "The Nightmare" also appear in "The Sound Of Poetry," a three-album set of compact discs/cassette tapes published by the International Library of Poetry; "The Balloon Man," as winner of a poetry contest, appeared in the February, 2003 issue of Writers' Journal; "Beamer's Battle Cry" was printed in "The Best Poems And Poets Of 2002," an anthology published by the International Library of Poetry in the spring of 2003.

Uncle Tim's Bridge, Wellfleet, MA
Photo by E. G. Pizzella

WORDBRIDGE

What words are best in common speech
To tell of one's devotion?
What phrase is there within one's reach
To bridge the widest ocean?

This query plunged me deep in thought
And answer did demand.
At first it seemed that I was caught,
Then came, "I understand."

AURHOR'S COMMENT: I chose the title of this piece as the title of the entire collection because, to me, poetry is the means or "bridge" by which the passions and emotions of the poet are transported to the hearts of his readers.

AMENDING THE GENDER OF GOD

An issue's been raised that strikes me as odd
And which here I'm inclined to expose.
Liberals now question the gender of God
And revisions of scripture propose.

Male reference to God we're urged to amend
By those who would dictate the norm,
That feminist feelings we may cease to offend
And to whims of correctness conform.

That God is in scripture depicted as male
Should never be seen as a slight.
Those ruled by emotions so tender and frail
Ought not to be judged in the right.

To some such distortions spawn infinite joy,
As they romp in the City of Oz,
But those with good sense they simply annoy
And to testy rebuke give just cause.

God is a spirit, I'm sure we all know,
So the issue's essentially moot.
What blessing does changing His image bestow,
For He wears neither dress nor a suit?

We know little of supernatural traits,
So on traits that we know we rely.
Unfamiliar perfection thus necessitates
That familiar descriptions apply.

So when to the deity we may ascribe
Styles which to gender relate,
Our object is just the unknown to describe,
Not to substantive policy state.

Why tarnish that age-honored image above
With labels born of false pride?
Let us instead reflect His great love,
Divisive minutia aside.

We live in a land where majority rules,
Where the few have a right to dissent,
But that doesn't mean we must paint ourselves fools,
So that frivolous feelings may vent.

I'll grant we must level the playing field
And for equality valiantly strive,
But if to extremists reason must yield,
At least let the classics survive.

Has the majority will relinquished its role,
So the lunatic fringe may now take control?

AUTHOR'S COMMENT: One morning in 1995, I was listening to the radio and heard a news report about a feminist group that was protesting about the male characterization of God in the bible and was advocating a revision of the scriptures. I became incensed, wrote this poem and submitted it to Brad Davis, a conservative talk-show host on WDRC radio in Hartford, Connecticut. Brad liked it and read on the air as part of his morning show.

ADAM'S RIB

In the Garden of Eden, they'd frequently stroll,
Discussing the news of the day.
On one such occasion God took control
And to Adam this did He say:

"I'm inclined to provide you a mate,
Who'll attend to each personal need.
Never depressed or irate,
Your insatiable ego she'll feed.

Blessed with beauty beyond compare,
She'll comply with your every command.
Your tribulations she'll readily share
And in every pursuit lend a hand."

"But what price will you demand, Sir?"
Adam asked with a cynical sneer.
"An arm and a leg," was the answer,
Which the mortal considered too dear.

Yet by the offer was Adam enticed
And this clever response did he render;
"Your goods are much overpriced,
But as payment a rib will I tender!"

Thus was the mortal's rib taken
And a delicate female produced.
Some say the man was mistaken;
Others say he indeed got a boost.

With amazement the damsel was greeted,
Her appearance too good to believe.
It was dusk when the job was completed,
Which explains why she was named Eve.

The error was seen in due time
And became Adam's primary sin,
For how could he think she would climb
Above what she had previously been.

All of which proves, when a bargain is sought
And the price of the item's reduced,
It usually follows that what has been bought
Is something quite cheaply produced.

The biblical facts herein disclosed
Basic lessons should clearly evoke,
That to equal rights let our minds not be closed,
But recall that a *rib* is a joke.

AUTHOR'S COMMENT: Mike Livingston is a union official, who worked in a neighboring office. He was an extremely pleasant chap with a wonderful sense of humor and would frequently come into my office and tell us jokes. One day he came in and told us the joke, which is the centerpiece of this poem. I just couldn't resist the challenge to turn it into a poem.

SONNET OF SANITY

The secret of life, I've finally learned,
Is to want what you have, what your labors have earned.
Repress all concern for things to obtain,
For unsatisfied wants give rise to much pain.

Life, I'm now sure, is a devious plot
To induce us to covet what we haven't got,
To batter us down each treacherous mile.
The answer is simple: bounce back with a smile!

Accept what is given and know when to battle.
Think for yourself; don't imitate cattle!
Pay little heed to what wise men profess
And never be lured by what rich folk possess.

If you follow these rules, I'm sure you will find
All your friends will describe you as *"Out of your mind!"*

Photo by E. G. Pizzella

CANINE MENDACITY

In my youth I was nurtured with a strict unbending rule,
One with which I vowed my children I would rear;
"It's forbidden to prevaricate, to deceive and try to fool,
For those who do, I'm sad to say, eternal pain must fear."

There's no doubt this worthy edict has acquired global fame
And its adherents in defense to any length would go.
Did not Shelley in his poetry rightfully proclaim
That *"Truth is beauty,"* which is *"all ye need to know?"*

But an exception to this maxim is also now well known
And its unexplained survival is enough to make me sick.
The mendacity of canines, prone and dormant, we condone,
Which forms the basis of a bone I'd like to pick.

Why of all the creatures, who inhabit mother earth,
Was Man's reputed friend in shame so rudely thrust?
This noble being, well endowed with dignity and worth,
Has been demeaned and thus is now deserving of mistrust.

A precept, which with reason cannot possibly comply,
Is that which whimsically permits "*a sleeping dog to lie.*"

AUTHOR'S COMMENT: As you can see, puns are one of my favorite
forms of humor.

A SURGICAL ALTERNATIVE

To a doctor with reluctance did I go,
For at the moment I was feeling very ill.
He examined me with care from head to toe,
Then wept a tear and handed me his bill.

When I begged him to tell me what was wrong,
He replied that a surgeon I must see.
With his advice I was bound to go along,
If from pain I desired to be free.

To the surgeon I accordingly proceeded
And x-rays of my chest were taken twice.
I was told that drastic surgery was needed,
But I confessed that I couldn't pay the price.

"Forget the operation," the skilled technician said,
"I'll just retouch the x-rays then instead!"

ETYMOLOGY

For my use of strange expressions I've been chided,
Which comes to me, of course, as no surprise.
Is one who caters to his mistress called *"misguided?"*
Such linguistic slights-of-hand give me a rise.

I'm enthralled by esoteric connotations
And by the games, which with words the witty play.
Puns to me are celestial incantations
And semantics are what brighten up my day.

This brings me to a matter of concern,
Relating to a rather common word.
Its derivation I'd do anything to learn
And thus to you this question I've referred:

If *"displeased"* is by the word *"disgruntled"* meant,
Does that mean that if I'm *"gruntled"* I'm *"content?"*

AUTHOR'S COMMENT: The first time I used the word "disgruntled" was in 1951. In 1950 my parents purchased a new Chevrolet sedan. This was the first time they ever owned a new car, all of their previous vehicles having been purchased as used. A short time after they bought the car they experienced a problem with its automatic transmission and they brought it back to the dealer to be repaired under the terms of the warranty. Sometime later the same problem recurred, but, when they brought it back to the dealer, they were told that they would have to pay for the repairs, because the warranty had expired. I was assigned the task of writing a letter of complaint to General Motors.

In my letter I contended that the warranty still applied, because the transmission had not been properly repaired on the first occurrence. I was upset with the dealer's calloused attitude and I began the letter by stating that my parents were the "disgruntled" owners of a newly purchased 1950 Chevrolet sedan and then went on to recite the facts. We received an immediate response and the company honored the warranty. I am firmly convinced that it was my use of the word "disgruntled" that did the trick.

AMERICA'S MAYOR

He was a principled, no-nonsense kind of guy,
As tough as any man in politics could be,
The mayor of a city that reaches upward to the sky
With millions, who persevere and prize their liberty.

He was thought by liberal minds to lack compassion
And for this reason many thought he didn't care.
The events of nine-eleven cast him suddenly in fashion,
As he became the world's most celebrated mayor.

Widows did he comfort and grieving families of the dead.
At the side of rescue workers dauntlessly he stood.
Hope and deep concern flowed from everything he said.
His message was of faith, of strength and brotherhood.

The spirits of his people did he tirelessly lift,
As he offered his assistance wherever there was need.
Calm, courageous leadership was his most precious gift,
Patently revealed in his every word and deed.

It sometimes takes misfortune to with clarity disclose
The merit that in statesmen may abundantly repose.

AUTHOR'S COMMENT: When our country's most populous city was brutally attacked by terrorists on September 11, 2001, I was profoundly impressed by the fortitude, courage, compassion and leadership exhibited by Mayor Rudy Giuliani and I was thus inspired to take pen to paper.

ARS GRATIA ARTIS

[Latin for "Art For The Sake Of Art"]

Many precious gifts has the Lord bestowed on Man;
Of this there cannot be the slightest doubt.
But that which most illuminates His mystifying plan
Is the one whose praises I now boldly shout.

Surely art is His most cherished and beneficial gift
And in bestowing it the artist is His hand.
Its purpose is Man's soul to edify and lift
And God's obscure divinity to better understand.

Art expresses love in its most pure and simple form
And proceeds from its maker's very core.
Not to standard modes does it in consequence conform,
But wily whim and impulse would explore.

A lesson from the artist are we thus compelled to take
And in those yet untested may it kindle rampant fire,
That art is created for naught but its own sake
And not simply to please those who would admire.

The work of an artist is the essence of his love,
Reflecting the glory of Him who reigns above.

AUTHOR'S COMMENT: Art in essence is the external expression of
the artist's innermost passions.

BEAMER'S BATTLE CRY

The terrorist attack of Nine-Eleven
Will fester in our memory through the years,
When those, whose profanity shocked heaven,
With malice sought to escalate our fears.

Many are the heroes who evolved from that event,
Their images emblazoned on our mind.
Can there be any doubt that they were heaven-sent
With valor among mortals hard to find?

Courageous were the passengers aboard Flight 93,
Who hearkened unto Beamer's brave command.
They epitomize the spirit that's kept our country free
And merit everlasting honor for their stand.

Their challenge was to save our way of life
And, where they left off, we must carry on.
Let us dedicate ourselves to freedom's strife,
As the armor of liberty we don.

May the battle cry that spurred them on, "Let's roll,"
Be etched indelibly on every righteous soul!

AUTHOR'S COMMENT: This was one of the most courageous manifestations of brotherly love that could be imagined. It was truly Christ-like. I sent this poem to the organizers of the Flight 93 Memorial.

HAPPINESS FOR HIRE

When life is with a critic's eye objectively reviewed,
The multitude of hours filled with sadness and travail
Exceed and far outweigh, one with candor must conclude,
The fleeting joys which on occasion happily prevail.

Such disproportion I address, aspiring thus to lift
The spirit of the human hoards, who for contentment strive,
Hoping that this meager, but well intentioned gift
Will root within their bosoms and keep will to live alive.

That the value of lofty themes we frequently extol,
I would be the first to publicly concede,
And, though earthly goods and riches should never be our goal,
That oft they fill the hapless breach is commonly agreed.

Though *"money can't buy happiness"* is etched in solid stone,
No official edict would preclude a short term loan.

LEGAL ASPECTS

"The law is an ass," is a serenade
I've heard, but believe is untrue.
Mistakes have been made
In the lawyering trade,
But let's place the blame where it's due.

Laws are just rules to which we resort,
When things go completely awry.
But lawyers distort,
Misusing the Court,
Citing laws that don't even apply.

The contention I make by way of defense
Should be stressed in all law school classes.
Our laws do make sense,
If we drop all pretense,
It's the lawyers themselves who are asses.

AUTHOR'S COMMENT: During my first year of law school, while I was researching a legal problem, I came across the expression, "the law is an ass." This was a commentator's reaction to a court decision that seemed to make no sense at all. It struck me as the worthy subject of a poem.

Photo by E. G. Pizzella

THE BALLOON MAN

Little hearts beat rapidly, as wide eyes squint and stare
At the motley globes that dance above his head.
He's the man who hawks balloons at every country fair,
For whom the sickest child would leave his bed.

Something very special about those vivid hues
Deprives youthful oglers of control.
As if he were a magnet and they wore metal shoes,
This huckster draws their body and their soul.

He'll organize his wares and hum a cheerful tune,
As he settles where he'll easily be found.
With a flourish, he'll release a brilliant red balloon
To lure the neighboring youngsters that abound.
The crimson sphere soars skyward and quite soon
An enthusiastic crowd has gathered 'round.

The process he'll repeat with blue and white.
Then purple, pink and green leap up with zest.
A dark skinned boy, who flanked him on the right,
Asked if black balloons rise upward like the rest.
The man let loose the black one he held tight
And with it this profound advice expressed:

"It's not the colors of balloons, my boy, that count;
It's what's inside that makes those critters mount."

AUTHOR'S COMMENT: When I attended one of my grandson's
First Communion ceremony, the priest who presided spoke about
the need for brotherly love and told the youngsters the story of the
balloon man. I was so moved by this simple but profound anecdote
that, when I arrived home, I immediately started work on this poem.

A NAUTICAL PARADOX

A man, who had sailed on a boat,
Disembarked with rubbery knees,
For the bob and weave of his float
Had caused him seasickness disease.

When at last his feet touched on land,
He bellowed like one who's insane.
Not a soul could his cries understand.
"A paradox," he'd loudly exclaim.

A passerby tugged at his sleeve
And queried what this was about.
"Is this an attempt to deceive?
What's this paradox of which you shout?"

Tongue in cheek, pointing seaward, he'd say,
"Those two matching piers in the bay!"

Photo by E. G. Pizzella

THE EYE OF A NEEDLE

Through the eye of a needle with much greater ease,
It's been said that a camel will pass,
Than a rich man into paradise squeeze,
Thus condemning the affluent class.

It's assumed all the rich have broken the rules
To garner their power and pelf;
That they've bunkoed the rest of us frivolous fools
In aggressive advancement of self.

Why does accumulation of wealth
Conjure visions of moral decay?
Can't someone be rich who has properly dealt
And observed all the rules on the way?

If those well endowed are destined for hell,
Then do paupers in merit excel?

WHAT GOVERNMENT GIVES

Democrats claim that they're helping the poor
By distributing funds that taxes have raised.
Entitlements thus make up the core
Of programs for which they seek to be praised.

They would have us believe they act out of care,
That their labors are spurred by deepest concern,
That they're simply assisting rich folks to share
And that ulterior motives they zealously spurn.

Their purpose, in truth, is to garner more votes
By creating dependents hooked on the dole.
Thus each flaming liberal his efforts devotes
To growing the budget out of control.

When election time comes, they boast of their deeds,
Taking pride in the hand-outs they've sponsored and passed.
They gloat that the system has met people's needs,
But demand that the spending yet be surpassed.

Be not misled by what glib liberals say,
For what government gives, it must first take away.

AUTHOR'S COMMENT: This is the key factor which those who
advocate socialistic policies and entitlements frequently overlook.

CALPURNIA'S DREAM

Dear distraught Calpurnia! Painful is thy woe,
For knotted are thy innards as thy spouse prepares to go.
Beg, persuade, appeal
And, if thou must, reveal
Departure's fatal consequence, which thou alone doth know.

"Beware the ides of March," did soothsayer proclaim,
Predicting that disaster would extinguish that rare flame,
Which in statesmanship excelled
And by treachery would be felled
And whose radiant accomplishments historians would acclaim.

Call upon thy wit! Use every ploy at thy command
To gain thy master's confidence and make him understand
The peril that's in store,
The betrayal and the gore,
Soon to be administered by once a friendly hand.

The provinces secured and many laurels earned,
He crossed the fabled Rubicon and in triumph he returned.
Anarchy he ended,
As to government he tended,
And from bellicose pursuits to peaceful ventures Caesar turned.

Benignly all his enemies he pardoned and forgave,
Those who would have killed him, both nobleman and knave.
This none before had done,
When victory had been won,
And proved a grievous error that led him to his grave.

From dissidents in the senate there were murmured hints of scorn,
As from fear and jealousy sedition had been born.
The gods placed Caesar's fate
In the hands of troubled mate,
Who, trembling from a nightmare, awoke that fateful morn.

Oh prophetic wife! If he'd but heeded thy alarm,
'Twould surely have saved both him and Rome from harm.
In slumber didst thou "murder" cry,
And calloused fate sought to defy,
Attempting to divert him with trickery and charm.

Wailing ghouls in streets appeared and tales of horror spread,
As belching graves, like vomit, expelled their rotting dead.
On clouds fought legions toe to toe,
Drizzling crimson blood below,
As groans of dying men gave rise to fear and dread.

Choruses of blinding flashes danced through somber skies,
Tumultuously applauded by moans and shrieking cries.
Phantoms passed without a word,
While lamentations could be heard,
Mourning victims of the mayhem in the process of demise.

Dispatched were priests in flowing robes to offer sacrifice
And mighty Caesar paused, awaiting their advice.
Absent heart in slaughtered beast
Worried him not in the least,
Who, casting risk aside, cast weighted dice.

To ominous predictions Caesar gave no ear,
For haughty pride precluded him from cowering in fear.
Deaf to every suppliant sound,
To the senate he was bound,
That morbid dreams and visions might not deter career.

"The death of lowly beggars illumines not the sky,
But with brilliance heavens blaze when mighty princes die."
Such did loving wife impart,
Which flowed directly from the heart,
And moved the great one wisely to reply:

"A coward's deaths are numbered by the score.
The valiant die but once and then no more."
To all but duty he was blind,
Yet she would try to change his mind
And other methods of persuasion cautiously explore.

She spoke to him of power, his future goals and needs,
The weakness of supporters and suspicion's budding seeds.
On reason she relied
And there urged him to abide,
Reminding him that treachery from envy oft proceeds.

At last did Caesar yield to the prayers of his mate,
Deferring his departure and matters of the state.
A message he would send
By Decius, his good friend,
That his appearance in the senate he'd decided to abate.

To his messenger alone did he disclose the reason.
"By wifely dream my decease is clearly now in season.
In sleep did she my statue view,
Which blood from many spouts did spew
And, in it bathing hands, did many join the treason."

Thus was noble monarch made the prisoner of his house,
Sheepishly submitting to the pleas of doting spouse.
But such was not to be,
For deceit would set him free
And the brilliant flame of greatness shortly douse.

Now Decius, who was cunning and clever in extreme,
Established at the outset that he knew well how to scheme.
That "Rome must its survival draw
From Caesar's vitals red and raw,"
He convincingly proposed to be the meaning of the dream.

Then said the cruel pretender with sharp sarcastic tone,
"If the reason for thy absence from the senate should be known,
Thou without a doubt would be
The butt of clownish mockery,
Unbecoming one so noble, who would occupy the throne."

In yet another ploy did Decius deftly then engage,
Announcing the inception of a new and royal age,
For "Roman Senate of renown
Is to vote the King a crown
And the effect of a postponement will be difficult to gauge."

The master was persuaded thus the senate to attend
By the calculated fawning of a most deceitful friend.
Turning regal mind aside
By chicanery and pride,
A courier brought lofty Caesar to his lowly end.

By the hands of fickle friends was the luminary slain
And, as he reeled from each assault, one horrid truth was plain;
For steel there was no need
To make his body bleed,
For the sight of each assassin sufficed his blood to drain.

Brutus! Cassius! Casca! Know ye what you've done?
Trebonius! Metellus! There's no place left to run!
Enormous is the cost
Of what the world has lost
And naught but bloody vengeance have your seditious efforts won.

The lesson to be learned from these events is crystal clear.
It's no disgrace at times to yield reluctantly to fear.
'Tis better to retreat,
Than submit to sure defeat,
For only by survival can one later reappear.

Observe the plaintive pleadings of a dedicated wife,
Which in the end effectively can save a husband's life.
Pride impervious, we know,
Did abet the fatal blow,
While credence might have spared both him and mortal strife.

As to flattery, be not duped or gullibly misled
By those who would selfishly try to turn one's head
With the clever words they speak,
While self-aggrandizement they seek,
Contriving that defenseless lambs to savage wolves be fed.

A warning foretold in the dream of a wife
Failed to defend her spouse from the knife.

AUTHOR'S COMMENT: I attended a performance of Shakespeare's "Julius Caesar" at the Hartford Stage Company and found it so moving that when I came home I could not wait to memorialize what I had seen. The result was this piece, as well as "The Power Of A Eulogy," which can be found on page 39.

THE LESSON

"Terrorists epitomize what's evil in this world,"
Announced a teacher boldly to her class,
"And our flag must therefore ever fly unfurled,
That such purveyors of evil may not pass."

"What's the purpose of evil," asked a child.
"It's to show us by contrast what is good."
Not for an instant was the teacher riled,
And without a doubt the youngster understood.

The teacher had her class write "evil" on their chests
And then before a mirror had them stand.
Most demonstrative was this of all her many tests,
Evoking the reaction that was planned.

'Twas a lesson that she often had rehearsed,
And one which with relish she would give,
For it's only when *evil* is reversed
That benevolence and human spirit *live*.

What was taught them they'd not very soon forget,
As they grieved for precious lives cut short.
Let there thus be no scintilla of regret,
When to war against the devil we resort.

Those who clamor endlessly for peace
Make demands that exhibit little sense,
For while attacks on the foe they say should cease,
They offer no plan for our defense.

The ravings which from pacifists arise,
If heeded, will hasten our demise.

AUTHOR'S COMMENT: I wrote this when the World Trade Center was attacked by Islamic terrorists. Little did I know then how aptly it would apply fourteen years later with the threats posed by ISIS.

IMPRESSIONS OF MY LADY

(Based on Dante's sonnet to Beatrice)

When to new acquaintances my lady I present,
The effects of the encounter are unique.
She's irresistibly disarming, so attractive and content,
That flippant tongues their idle chatter dare not speak.

The aura of her beauty so captivates the soul
That eyes must turn aside, her luster to evade.
The unprepared observer must fight for self-control,
When any slight approach to her is made.

Humbly she maintains her meek and mild demeanor,
In spite of overwhelming flattery and praise.
Blessed exceedingly are those honored to have seen her,
For pristine and most celestial are her ways.

The impression she creates, whene'er she passes by,
From strangers, struck with awe, evokes a sigh.

AUTHOR'S COMMENT: I found Dante's sonnet to be so beautiful that I was anxious, not only to translate it, but to present it in poetic form.

Ed Pizzella, as Victor Velasco, and Gail Gregory, as Mrs. Banks, in "Barefoot In The Park" at the Connecticut Cabaret in Berlin, CT

ACTORS ALL

Actors, I fear, are unjustly portrayed
And no doubt they are due for a break.
Perhaps it's because a role's said to be *"played,"*
That an actor's condemned as a fake.

"What is this endeavor?" a skeptic might ask
Of one numbed by the fatal disease.
Well, the answer is *"causing a difficult task*
To be done with the greatest of ease."

Acting is not, as some might suppose,
Just putting on make-up and making believe,
But a skill that's selectively lavished on those,
Who know not how to deceive.

An actor, in truth, emotes from within
In order to sway from without.
Each role demands that he don a new skin
To remove any possible doubt.

Drawn by insatiable hunger and thirst,
An audience longs to be fed,
But its needs cannot be met until first
By conviction the actor is led.

This penchant requires immense concentration,
With control and attention to minute detail.
Timing's essential and much preparation;
And all must combine, or the actor will fail.

In his art an actor invests all his soul;
Empathy's what he seeks to create.
To completely convince is his ultimate goal,
Which requires much more than just talent innate.

If this nebulous term I should seek to define,
I'd have to profess with a great deal of verve:
"An actor must live every move, every line
To so noble a title deserve."

And is it not true that we in our lives
Must act out a role every day?
Whether at work, or as husbands or wives,
Nothing's done well, if not done that way.

This worthy pursuit should not be defamed,
For *"The world is a stage!"* Has it not been proclaimed?

AUTHOR'S COMMENT: I became deeply involved in community
theatre on a dare in 1966. For the next thirty-six years I performed
roles, many of them leading roles, in more than one hundred
theatrical productions. I also produced and directed a number of

shows, until I retired from this avocation in 2003. This poem has its roots in my profound love of theatre. In 2014, I published a theatrical memoir entitled "The Versatility Of Chairs," which can be ordered in book stores or on the internet.

SLEEPING BEAUTY

There's beauty in all things on land and sea,
Though at times it may be difficult to see it.
Obscured in jagged rock and wrinkled tree,
It tests the artist's skill to simply free it.

As nature its marvels surreptitiously conceals,
The tasty nut seeks refuge in its shell.
So, lurking stealthily in motley burrs and peels
Are phenomenal delights no words can tell.

In the fiber of the canvas linger hibernating forms,
As from tubes to be disgorged wait vivid hues.
When spirit moves the artist, who with brush in hand performs,
The brilliance of his work in finality ensues.

The diamond masks its glitter in a dull and shapeless mass,
Suppressing gleaming facets deeply buried in its core.
Precision in its cutting is what gives this jewel its class,
As weaned are golden nuggets by the smelter from the ore.

What artful charms and passions lie dormant in the word,
Condemned to mute and inarticulate frustration?
Yet from a poet's lips sheer eloquence is heard,
When simple language is adorned by inspiration.

In murky depths the precious pearl in oyster shell matures,
The product of prolonged and intensive irritation,
While the crystal's stunning sparkle dolomite obscures,
Evading Man's intrusive adulation.

Amorphous is the clay that once spawned humankind,
Yet a myriad of designs therein restlessly repose.
It's only when the craftsman shares the vision in his mind
That their splendor they may to the world expose.

In the strident, deafening discord of earth's cacophony,
The wailing wind, the ocean's roar, the howling of the plains,
The composer hears the music of a perfect symphony,
Sweetly swelling in melodic, dulcet strains.

Demurely hides the statue, snugly sheltered in the stone,
There clandestinely secreted since creation.
As patience slowly withers, it hears the chisel's tone
And anxiously awaits its liberation.

So it is with all the gifts by which we're blessed,
Each stalk, each twisted branch, each patch of earth.
Preordained is their essence in art to be expressed,
Thus revealing nature's cache of ample worth.

Yea, pulchritude glows latent in all that we behold,
Relentlessly resisting exploitation,
And yet another boon to be equally extolled
Is the talent that's employed in revelation.

The artist's job is not to make what's new,
But just to clear away what blocks our view.

AUTHOR'S COMMENT: One evening I was tuned into a television program about the art of sculpture. There was a segment about Michelangelo in which they displayed and commented on the David and some of his other works. I said to myself, "No human being could possibly create such perfection. Only God could have performed those feats." Then I thought, "Maybe God did create them and concealed them in the stone, until this clever guy came along and set them free." It was that seed that gave birth to this piece, as well as "David's Debut," which can be found on page 147.

THE PINBALL MACHINE

"Got some quarters, Dad?" I'd heard that voice before,
Then a hand reached in my pocket to explore.
"Quickly or I'll lose my place!"
A harried look crept o'er his face
And seconds later he was bounding out the door.

This occurrence was in all respects routine;
Quite normal both for parent and for teen.
I'd been the object of a raid
By my son in the arcade
And he was rushing back to torment his machine.

He had mastered that oblique pinball device,
Which he held firmly in a grip much like a vice.
He would whisper, push and roll,
Attempting vainly to control
Globes of metal unreceptive to advice.

He'd pull the pin and then release it with a twist.
I marveled at the subtle revolution of his wrist.
His concentration was immense,
His body rigid, stiff and tense,
As though nothing else on earth did now exist.

Propelled directly to the high point of the field,
Its thrust designed to seek the highest yield,
The missile mounted the incline,
Where its speed would soon decline
And the path of its return would be revealed.

Its forward motion having now been all but spent,
The ball commenced its unpredictable descent.
Undecided where to go,
It just wandered to and fro,
And none of those who watched knew where 'twas bent.

Now this is where a player's skill is seen,
As o'er this odd contrivance he will lean,
And gently tap upon the side,
Surreptitiously to guide
The projectile to score heavy on the screen.

I observed him, as he whistled with a lilt
To prove that what he did was without guilt.
Excessive force is taboo.
He must never overdo,
Or the game he will forfeit by a tilt.

The random path of each descending sphere
Is reminiscent of the life we hold so dear,
Bouncing helplessly around
With no idea of where we're bound,
And hoping fervently that luck will interfere.

The spheroid is befuddled, as it's jolted here and there,
And, even though inert, it seems likely to dispair.
Without the slightest clue
As to direction to pursue,
To its errant course our lives ironically compare.

The features, which so entice me to this game,
Are those which in our lives appear the same,
For to a great degree
It mirrors life's futility,
And the fact that for so many it lacks aim.

As we stumble on our way devoid of grace,
Some being up above o'ersees our pace
And, like the boy in command,
Offers us a helping hand
That we, in life's obstructed course, may find our place.

AUTHOR'S COMMENT: On one occasion, when I took my family on a trip to Hampton Beach in New Hampshire, we stopped at an amusement park with a penny arcade. My son, Mike, was in his early teens and became obsessed with the pinball machines. While we were walking around checking things out, he would periodically run over to me and frantically beg for coins to feed the machines. His unmitigated enthusiasm compelled me to author this piece.

THE POWER OF A EULOGY

"Men are survived by the evil that they do,
While the good is oft interred with their bones."
So spoke Antony of him who Brutus slew
In provoking and inflammatory tones.

To the assassins he appealed that he might eulogize his friend,
But Caius Casius was suspicious of his aim.
The attributes of Caesar he was told he could commend,
Provided that against them he would speak no word of blame.

In yielding to his plea, they exacted a condition,
Fearful that the mob he might incite.
They required him to say that he spoke with their permission,
Or else they would have barred him from the rite.

"I've come to bury Caesar, not to praise him," he avowed.
"Wild ambition," he charged, *"was Caesar's grievous fault."*
With calculated eloquence he spirited the crowd
And against seditious slayers launched a punitive assault.

"Men of honor are they all," he exclaimed with tongue in cheek
And Caesar's triumphs he pretended to rebuke as evil deeds.
The anger of the rabble did he with cunning seed and pique,
Pointing out the wounds from which the blood of genius bleeds.

Countless, senseless apertures, scarlet, tongueless, dumb,
Yet by ingratitude and treason taught persuasively to speak,
Inflicted in ambush, caused a giant to succumb
And on the vile conspirators did bloody vengeance wreak.

From the escalating tumult the culprits fled in haste,
Ironically pursued by those they'd sought to please.
From battle to battle they persistently were chased,
Until each rogue in infamy was humbled to his knees.

Thus a eulogy delivered with the murderers' accord
Proves once again that artful words cut deeper than the sword.

AUTHOR'S COMMENT: I was deeply moved by the seditious eloquence of Marc Antony, who, with artful language, was able to incite his audience without arousing the suspicion of the assassins, until it was too late to stop him. For information about what inspired the author to write this poem refer to the comment following "Calpernia's Dream" on page 23.

THE PRACTICE OF THE DOVE

Man boasts of many attributes bestowed by God above,
Of intellect and reason and the act of making love.
In bi-sexual reproduction he takes pride
And biologists support and take his side,
But by far more advantageous is the practice of the dove.

Man's modus operandi, more objective minds contend,
Is clumsy and confusing with results that may offend.
So, let's compare the human way
With birds preferring eggs to lay
To find out if the human method's one we can defend.

That the hen extrudes her fertile egg with ease is very plain,
While human birth's attended with excruciating pain.
Yet the chick's no less endowed,
Of which progenitors are proud.
It's no wonder that our mode is viewed by some with much disdain.

From fertile egg evolves a product fully as complex
As a child produced in woman by the act of human sex,
But with people things will vary,
For the couple now must marry,
Converting them in consequence to psychiatric wrecks.

Among the lower primates, the male participant is free
To go about his business in total liberty.
By nature he's not duty bound
To offer help or hang around
And the pregnant female's foremost in his discharge to agree.

But in human reproduction, to which I've previously referred,
A binding oath, if not expressed, is frequently inferred,
For once the womb is seeded,
It's felt commitment's needed
And subsequently on the male are obligations thus conferred.

The lengthy term required in humans for gestation
Creates a rather awkward and dependent situation.
Resulting need for male support
Induces female to resort
To badgering her helpless mate in vile humiliation.

The male of every species is of similar design.
His function is to propagate, not socialize and dine.
He prefers attachments fleeting
And after sex is found retreating.
Toward permanent relations only women do incline.

AUTHOR'S COMMENT: Many years ago I purchased a house from the estate of a deceased English teacher. When I viewed the property prior to the closing, I found that in the house were a number of book cases crammed with old and interesting books. As the closing date approached, the broker assured me that the heirs would remove all the books. I was stunned. I said, "they needn't bother. I'd be happy to take the property in its existing, cluttered condition." I thus became the owner of those fascinating books. I subsequently picked up an old volume, dusted it off and began reading. This was an old medical treatise written by a man who was both a doctor and a preacher. In each chapter he would discuss a particular medical procedure and inject his moralistic views. I turned to the chapter on reproduction and was both amused and astonished by what I read, which is the essence of this poem.

ALYSSA'S TOAD

To the shallow pond behind the house she went,
A see-through plastic cup within her hand.
On exploration it's doubtless she was bent
With youthful joy unbridled in command.

Her curiosity was handsomely rewarded
And she returned with her deeply cherished prize.
The beauty of this child is thus recorded
With awe and innocence reflected in her eyes.

With happiness impossible to measure
And trust which words lack power to explain,
She lifts up to the lens her tiny treasure,
As proof that her quest was not in vain.

Credit for this scene to God alone is owed,
The unveiling of Alyssa's new found toad.

AUTHOR'S COMMENT: When my granddaughter, Alyssa, was three or four years old, I took her to visit a friend who had a pond behind his house. There were some older children with us and they wanted to play near the edge of the pond. Alyssa took a plastic cup with her to see if she could find some interesting water creatures. Fortunately, I had my trusty camera with me and, when she returned with her precious find, I snapped this picture. I later entered it in a contest sponsored by a national digital photo magazine and it was published.

THE BEST LAID PLANS

The horrors of September in the year Two Thousand One
Revealed a multitude of heroes hidden in our midst,
Who reflect our country's greatness in all that they have done
And gave that evil venture a true ironic twist.

From the "apple" of our eye were lives and structures cruelly torn
In an effort to destroy what those who hate can't comprehend,
But like mythology's Phoenix has our spirit been reborn
And we who've been assailed will savor victory in the end.

Police and firefighters, cooks and clerks and common folk,
All displayed outstanding courage in the cowardly attacks.
Though self-preservation one might think it would evoke,
To those in fear and peril they never turned their backs.

From every diverse group they joined to lend a helping hand
And from every distant corner flowed donations to the cause.
Proudly are the stars and stripes flown throughout the land
And in the process of revival there's not been the slightest pause.

From catastrophic mayhem arose a fact that's crystal clear,
That by God this great republic has abundantly been blessed,
For, though dastardly villains sought to humble us in fear,
Their attempt did to the world but expose our very best.

This clearly proves what Robert Burns would very likely say,
That *"The best laid plans o'mice and men aft [will] gang agley."*

AUTHOR'S COMMENT: Like so many others, I was traumatized by
the horrible events of September 11, 2001 and this is how I vented
my anguish.

COMMON STUFF

Greedy alchemists of old,
From metals that were clearly base,
Sought to manufacture gold
And thus their poverty erase.

Their experiments were doomed,
For nature's law would never yield.
From eyes with avarice consumed
Is true value oft concealed.

Not in substance is there worth,
But in unique, creative form.
Any product of the earth
Will to this simple rule conform.

What ancients sought and never found
Is not how metals may be changed,
But brilliant artworks that abound,
Made of stuff that's rearranged.

Priceless art is often wrought
From materials worth naught.

AUTHOR'S COMMENT: It always amazed me that, when we think about wealth, we focus on things that have intrinsic value, such as silver, gold and jewels, and we overlook the fact that there are many things of immense value, which are composed of substances which are practically worthless.

CONSIDER THE LILIES

[Based on Matthew 6:25 – 34]

Be not distressed about life's demands,
About what you shall drink or what you shall eat.
Leave these concerns in God's able hands,
For He will provide what's needed and meet.

Be assured that your heavenly Father doth care,
So dwell not on things that are clearly mundane.
Look at those creatures who soar in the air;
They sow not, nor reap, yet amply sustain.

For want of provisions birds are not sad.
Are you not of greater value than they?
And which of you, being anxious, can add
To the span of his life one single day?

Be not perplexed about what you shall wear.
Consider the lilies that grow in the field!
They toil not, nor spin, nor yet do they care,
For their beauty has heaven most seemly revealed.

In his glory King Solomon ne'er was arrayed
In attire as splendid as God has clothed these,
But if worthless weeds He's so comely displayed,
Why would He not seek His children to please?

Have faith, seek His kingdom and follow His path,
Lest impatience invite His judgment and wrath.
Your Father in heaven knows just what you need
And whatever's required to you will He cede.

AUTHOR'S COMMENT: The Biblical passage on which this poem is based is, in my opinion, one of the most powerful passages in scripture. The all too familiar, vivid and earthy comparisons present an irrefutable dialectic. It reminds me of a brilliant trial attorney making his most persuasive closing argument.

ELUSIVE LOVE

I've yearned for her these many years,
But scarcely does she heed.
Beholding her through salty tears,
I've bared my boundless need.

I've stalked her with persistence
And I've humbly begged and cried,
Yet the core of my existence
Casts me callously aside.

I've made myself so vulnerable,
I shudder at the thought.
Am I so vain and gullible
To think she can be caught?

Whimsically with me she toys,
As I expose my craving soul.
A victim of her cunning ploys,
I've lost my self-control.

If I should now disclose her name,
You'd think me quite absurd,
But I'm a poet without shame
And whom I covet is the word.

THE ERA OF THE DUCK

What animal's symbolic of the mores of today?
I rise with zeal to nominate the *duck,*
For the images the mention of this mindless *foul* convey
Exemplify how we have run amuck.

Misfeasance is excused in every instance
And reason's scorned, as feelings rule the day.
To temptation we offer no resistance,
As elitists dictate what we ought to say.

Approval of abortion is referred to as pro-choice
That consequential guilt we may discreetly hide.
Denigration of our country many critics loudly voice,
While they profit from the system they've decried.

As we *waddle* through the mire of self-indulgence,
Pleasure is the ruler we slavishly obey.
Spurned are discipline and good old common sense,
Lest rules and moral values block our way.

For ailments caused by smoking, it's big tobacco that we sue
And when shots are heard, the maker of the gun.
People bear no fault for the foolish things they do
And immense are the verdicts that are won.

His actions were condoned as an addiction,
When Clinton groped the women on his staff.
His ratings soared despite this predilection
And the legal implications of his gaffe.

Our declining culture glorifies evasion
And individual responsibility's taboo!
With agility we *duck* on each occasion,
When blame for our miscues might ensue.

Marriage has at last been redefined
And no longer requires different sexes.
Priorities have all been realigned
And the Ten Commandments are treated now as hexes.

Principles time-honored through the ages
Are callously discarded with a sneer.
Re-written are reams of history's pages,
Which with agendas of the left may interfere.

Liberals advocate unfettered use of drugs
And would euthanize both elderly and ill.
Meager sentences reward convicted thugs
And for every slight annoyance there's a pill.

Old Glory's burned in public without a trace of fear,
While our founders are the subject of attacks.
Judgments based on values completely disappear,
Like water shed from *well-oiled feathered backs*.

Many local jobs have been out-sourced
In order to enhance the bottom line.
Immigration laws no longer are enforced,
Since for many open borders are just fine.

Groundless litigation chokes the dockets of our courts,
As ill-gotten gains become our prey.
Steroid use has tarnished the repute of major sports
And violence becomes more prevalent every day.

Borrowing has risen to frightening extremes
And debt is among our greatest ills.
Frantic are our efforts to realize our dreams,
As we're relentlessly pursued by unpaid *bills*.

References to God are universally condemned
And prayer is banned in all the public schools.
Sexual promiscuity is now a stylish trend
And those who disagree are mocked as fools.

Contradiction and hypocrisy uncontested reign
Among those who should set a good example.
Integrity's deplored and goes quickly down the drain
For political advantage, which is ample.

And when conservatives bemoan such morbid facts,
The bleeding hearts are quick to call them *quacks*.

AUTHOR'S COMMENT: This piece effectively expresses many of my core conservative beliefs and writing it provided a vent for my frustrations.

THE ESSENCE OF DIPLOMACY

Recently, when I embraced my lover,
For, as yet, I haven't lost the spark,
Something very strange did I discover,
Which prompts me in this missive to remark.

What is it about hugging that has changed?
Hugs in days gone by were not a strain.
This pursuit has by time been rearranged
In ways that I find awkward to explain.

It's not that there's an increase in your weight, dear,
Or that your waistline to some extent has grown.
The situation's more deplorable than that, I fear,
So let the gruesome truth at last be known.

There's no appreciable expansion of your border,
It's simply that my arms have gotten shorter.

AUTHOR'S COMMENT: This piece was entered in a contest and won first prize.

Photo by E. G. Pizzella

BLUE AS THE PLEON

From Wells to Kennebunk to Biddeford Pool,
We scoured Maine's salty and serpentine shore.
Clear was the weather for the most part, but cool,
Offering marvelous ops for photos galore.

Then Harpswell, Beale's Island and old Popham Beach,
Pemiquid Point, Deer Isle, Boothbay;
To interesting places extending our reach
And pleasant were stops that we made on our way.

At Lubec the fog was a shutterbug's dream,
Giving lighthouse and bridge an ominous air.
Campobello Island was next to be seen,
Where FDR had his world famous lair.

To Eastport we headed with camera in hand,
Where we longed for elusive sun to appear.
There we would make our last digital stand,
Snapping photos we'd later at leisure revere.

We recalled feisty tugboats that sat by the pier.
Among them the Pleon, cocky and proud.
With multiple colors, bright, crisp and clear,
They then seemed to mock us, laughing out loud.

We looked forward to eye-catching buildings and boats,
All glistening and posed in a brilliant array,
But, chilled by the breeze, we both donned our coats
And the skies remained cloudy with grimacing gray.

Gone were the hues we'd seen there before
And the glitz in the past that had captured our gaze.
Spectacular subjects were either no more,
Or obscured by fog and a lackluster haze.

Drab was the town we were anxious to view
And the Pleon was monochrome, all painted blue.

AUTHOR'S COMMENT: My companion, Shirley, and I traveled many times to Eastport in Maine. We fell in love with the Maine coast with its many scenic peninsulas, islands and quaint harbors. Every time we arrived at Eastport we would look for our favorite nautical gem, the Pleon, a brightly painted multicolored tugboat. On our last trip the weather was dreary and we were disappointed to find that our prized tug was now painted a monochrome blue.

HAVEN ON THE LAKE

Nestled in a niche on Lake Ontario's northern shore
Is an oasis known to travelers as the Millhaven Inn,
Where those in search of solace may their wilted souls restore,
Escaping life's travails and hectic din.

Hollyhocks and lilies add zest to vibrant green,
As contently cattle graze in the leas across the road.
Leisurely immersed in the lush bucolic scene,
Weary patrons are invited to unload.

While the Amherst Island ferry its crisscross path does ply
Amid the bobbing sails that meander to and fro,
Beneath the water's surface a loon does nimbly fly,
Exploring hidden wonders that we will never know.

Enchanted by the twinkles that dot the rippled lake
And gently calmed by its constant ebb and flow,
From its clear crystal liquid inspiration do I take
And I happily return to barren fields that I must sow.

Here I breathe a sigh, as I quench my thirst for peace,
Praying that its bounty in my lifetime will not cease.

AUTHOR'S COMMENT: Shirley and I enjoy traveling in Canada, where we will frequently spend a few days at the Millhaven Inn, a lovely three hundred year old retreat located on the northern shore of Lake Ontario. There we immerse ourselves in the beauty of the lake and the bucolic scenery and we return, our spirits refreshed by the generous hospitality of Anita and Tony, our gracious hosts.

HIS EMPTY SHOES

Optimistic was their future, filled with hope and truly bright,
And they played their roles, observing all the cues.
Anxious for her welcome, when he came home at night,
By the door he would leave his empty shoes.

He went to work that morning. 'Twas a fair September day
In that teeming metropolis, where murderers were sent.
Never more would she see him, nor would she hear him say
How her warm embrace would his ecstasy foment.

Symbolizing commerce in the world's most famous city,
Twin towers stood erect, stabilized by metal and cement.
Never did she dream they'd be objects of her pity,
Nor that their sudden, cruel destruction she'd lament.

In this era of technology with billions earmarked for defense,
How could we our safety otherwise augment?
Our government, we're told, spares no reasonable expense
The willful slaughter of our neighbors to prevent.

Yet, aircraft came from nowhere to strike a fatal blow
And beams, once rigid, buckled, bowed and bent.
The caress of her husband nevermore would she know,
But his absence would she hence bitterly resent.

Many months have passed without her love's return
And marked with pain is each empty moment spent.
The details of his demise she has sadly yet to learn,
So futile fantasies does she aimlessly invent.

She's manufactured myths concerning what occurred
And the ways he might have made a safe descent.
But despite the lapse of time, she's received not a word,
Which immeasurably increases her torment.

He left her with a void that's colossal in its size,
So much to her existence had this loving mortal meant.
Whenever she thinks of him, she must dry her eyes
And she wears his empty shoes to feel content.

It's odd how foolish gestures can mean so very much,
As we strive to fill the void left by the absence of a touch.

AUTHOR'S COMMENT: After the terrorist attack of September 11, 2001, I heard this story and was so touched that I found it impossible to resist the urge to express the wife's remorse in poetry.

I LOVE A PARADE

In the distance we hear the rhythmic drumming
And, jumping to my feet, my pulse rate soars!
Hooray! The marching bands at last are coming,
And with them drill teams, majorettes and many corps.

My fragile heart palpitates and pounds
At the sight of floats and marchers in the street,
Their uniforms so colorful, the sounds,
And all in perfect step! God, what a treat!

The metallic wail of brass, the tuba's burp,
The deep staccato rumble of the drum;
Control of my emotions they usurp,
As to the wispy whine of woodwinds I succumb.

I'm dazed by Souza's stimulating strains,
The rhythm and the dulcet mellow tones.
Unconsciously I hum robust refrains,
Which seem implanted in the marrow of my bones.

In sync with the blaring music's beat
Is the symmetric sway of every head and arm,
Which combine with coordinated feet
To overwhelm with captivating charm.

The impulse to join them I resist,
But I find myself betrayed by tapping feet.
The imagined baton clenched in my fist
Proves that my hypnosis is complete.

As a child I was thrilled by a parade,
And my passion refuses yet to fade.

A LAWYER'S LAMENT

Lawyers everywhere are spawning litigation.
In many circles they're the movers and the doers
And recent cases, renowned throughout the nation,
Attest to their repute as avid suers.

Their Machiavellian traits did they reveal,
When McDonald's was caught within their trap.
Though the verdict was reduced upon appeal,
The beans were spilled when coffee seared a lap.

They sue wealthy firms that market cigarettes,
Obtaining judgments that number in the billions,
While subsidies from taxes hedge the bets
Of farmers who produce for Brown and Williams.

Their clients were aware that smoking kills,
Yet they continued to puff upon the weed.
Now they seek a bonus for their ills,
Relying on the law to intercede.

There are victims who everyday get shot
And there's no doubt that something must be done.
Those who pull the triggers have no pot,
So they sue the well heeled makers of the gun.

Now a problem that lawyers soon will face
And about which there is little they can do
Is that, if lawsuits maintain their current pace,
They'll be running out of parties they can sue.

THE RENDERING

A conundrum that sadly confronts us today
And hits us directly between the eyes
Is one for which we must certainly pay,
The problem of bloated bellies and thighs.

We all must avoid the junk food we crave,
For obesity's known to cause many ills.
It's an addiction that surely will lead to the grave
And one for which there aren't any pills.

To our rescue, alas, have attorneys now come,
As MacDonald's and Wendy's march bravely to court.
Purveyors of fat, no doubt, will succumb
To a new definition of what the law terms a tort.

My intent is not to unjustly demean,
But, when all's said and done, I smell a rat,
For, as the courts compel fast foods to be lean,
The wallets of lawyers will surely be fat.

Against those, who to millions french fries would feed,
Will fatuous verdicts now be decreed?

THE NIGHTMARE

From a nightmare I awoke,
Drained by overwhelming fright.
Fearing I had had a stroke,
I waited breathless for dawn's light.

Depressed, confused and insecure,
I felt I'd lost my will to live,
For I was absolutely sure
No more had fickle life to give.

What message did that dream convey
That caused me such concern;
That sages had no more to say
And there was nothing left to learn.

My ignorance no longer do I rue,
As daily I'm apprised of something new.

THE IDENTITY CRISIS

Many are concerned about who they really are,
So the Identity Crisis has become an epidemic.
Elusive are the symptoms, which appear to be bazaar
And cannot be explained by psychiatrist or medic.

The answer can be found in a place not very far.
Just look into a mirror and have a raucous laugh.
You need not be concerned, for you are who you are,
So focus on the inner you and eliminate the chaff.

That you are who you are is a concept unmistaken,
For everybody else, without a doubt, has been taken.

Photo by E. G. Pizzella

THE CAT AT MYSTIC COVE

There's a cat at Mystic Cove I'll not forget,
Though only fleeting moments elapsed when first we met.
Scampering from out the brush,
To and fro he'd gaily rush,
As though sporadically propelled by hidden jet.

Performing playful stunts much like a clown,
He'd socialize while flitting up and down.
Darting in the golden rod,
This rascal seemed to me quite odd,
For, though he was a tiger, he yet was cocoa brown.

He was congenial, high spirited and proud,
And with whiskers abundantly endowed.
Eyes of deeper green
I have never seen,
Nor markings so colorful and loud.

Thinking he'd not linger in one spot,
My camera I unleashed to take a shot.
When I asked the scamp to pose,
In my lens he poked his nose.
Now I'm haunted by the image that I got.

That frisky feline flirt I'll not forget,
Nor the temptation to adopt him as my pet.
Though I maintained my self control,
He left his paw print on my soul,
As I continued on my way with fond regret.

AUTHOR'S COMMENT: One summer evening, I met my daughter, Laura, and her family at Mystic Cove on the Connecticut shoreline. We stopped at a take-out for an evening snack and then proceeded to take a leisurely walk along the shore, when suddenly this frisky feline leaped out of the brush and greeted us. He was very friendly and it seemed that he wanted to put on a show for us. When he approached me, I had my camera in my hand and I was amazed that I was able to capture this shot. I subsequently wrote a sequel entitled, "Inspired By The Mews." (pg. 220)

A LEGAL OPINION

It started with a burglar, who sued the victim of his theft
For injuries sustained when he broke in.
The judgment that was rendered left the guiltless man bereft,
While the thug was well rewarded for his sin.

Summarily expelled was a student starting fights,
So he brought suit against the Board of Education.
It was held that the vandal was deprived of precious rights,
For which he was awarded compensation.

Thieves held up a bank and, when a fusillade ensued,
A robber was killed in the confusion.
Judgment was recovered by his family, when they sued
For delay in providing a transfusion.

Decisions such as these make people wring their hands.
For the law the population's lost respect.
We apply legal principles no jurist understands,
So that no one need account for his neglect.

In days gone by a lawsuit was a matter of concern,
Nor was frivolity e'er welcomed in a court.
A liar, it was thought, in hell would surely burn,
And a courthouse was a place of last resort.

Shakespeare in his works said that lawyers should be "killed,"
For he recognized the plight that we now face.
His words, it seemed, with sarcasm and humor must be filled,
But extremes that we have witnessed make his case.

The legal system, all agree, is choked with litigation,
And there are just too many lawyers on the scene.
The Bard's proposal may indeed have been exaggeration,
But some accept his words for what they mean.

Perhaps such condemnation is too harsh, some have opined.
Barristers ought not be killed, but legally confined.

AUTHOR'S COMMENT: Although my avocation is writing, my vocation is that of a lawyer and one might think it odd that some of my poetry ("Flaw And Order," "A Lawyer's Lament," "Legal Aspects," "Professional Pride" and "The Rendering," as well as this piece) satirizes my profession. Having practiced law vigorously and continuously for fifty-eight years, these criticisms stem from my observation of what appears to me a gradual deterioration of professionalism, coupled with a startling increase of commercialism in this field. Regrettably, this downward progression seems to have paralleled the deterioration of our culture.

Photo by E. G. Pizzella

CURIOUS CONFLAGRATION

I shouted in excitement, "There's a fire!
We must flee the rampant flames that sear the brush!"
Gleaming crimson tongues that leap and never tire
Caused my adrenaline to flow and cheeks to flush.

"Sound the alarm! We're trapped in its all-consuming spread!"
I looked around and in amazement spied
The glow of incandescent amber mixed with red,
Which in a radiant deluge emersed the countryside.

"Is this the fiery finale bible prophecies portray,
Nature's ultimate incendiary flare,
The final brilliant bursts of life's fireworks display,
The cataclysmic end of all we share?"

"Hold on there, sir! Please keep your cool!
No need have we of water, trucks and hose.
'Tis the season we dub 'Fall,' you silly fool,
When foliage once verdant turns to rose."

I scanned the autumn blaze and caught my breath.
What master's this who wildly dabs the trees?
Yea, if I live a century 'til my death,
Ne'er shall I view such splendid hues as these.

Iridescent scarlet stains boughs previously green,
As pigments that would clash, now seem to blend.
Who's this demented artist so precocious, yet unseen?
Makes he of mottled woodland mortal enemy or friend?

Is this some neophyte who strives for worldly fame,
Whose chromatic indiscretions shake the norm?
A perfect being such emotions would restrain,
And to standards more conservative conform.

Fall hues reveal the genius of God's hand,
Which gratefully we view, yet fail to understand.

AUTOR'S COMMENT: I enjoy traveling and my companion and
I have made several tours of Vermont in early October. I was so
impressed by the fabulous colors of the foliage that I was inspired
to write this piece. At first, I titled it "Autumn Blaze," but I later
decided to add to its mystique by changing the title to "Curious
Conflagration."

Photo by E. G. Pizzella

UNDERCOVER

Judge a book not by its cover,
For 'neath its surface you'll discover
Endless knowledge, truths galore,
More facts than any brain can store;
Marvels one might not expect;
Food to nourish intellect;
Stories which from genius flow;
Scenes that in reflection glow;
More than one unread could know.

Within its pages you'll explore
What you've not seen or felt before,
Indeed what might ignite your core;
Verbal pictures bound to please;
Exotic places, fantasies
On mystic isles in distant seas;
Emotions mixed with glee and pain;
Ideas that brilliant minds retain
And inspiration may unchain;
Scripts that merit accolades;
Tales of famous men and maids;
Adventures, thrills and escapades;
Wisdom research oft dispenses;
Sights and sounds that stun the senses;
Psychic thrusts with no defenses;
History, science, incisive thought
By which your fancy may be caught;
All of which by words are wrought.

Such groups of letters, row on row,
Like seeds that farmers daily sow,
Beneath the cover barren lie,
Until we till them with our eye,
Whereupon they grow.

AUTHOR'S COMMENT: My objective here was to promote reading, which I believe is essential to the realization of the American dream. Reading educates and ignorance causes poverty.

THE SIGNIFICANCE OF SAUCERS

(or "Alimentary, My Dear Watson")

Aliens from outer space on earth one day did land
And offered all the folks they met a warm and friendly hand.
They seemed to have been sent by fate
Some lofty message to relate,
Which persistently they tried to make world leaders understand.

Their demeanor was congenial and they seemed to be sincere,
Though the purpose of their visit was in some respects unclear.
To converse became absurd,
For we could fathom not a word,
Since their vocal pitch was in a range too high for us to hear.

Communication, as a consequence, was carried on by sign
And, though primitive and cumbersome, this method worked just fine,
But we became a bit confused,
When abruptly they refused
To join us in our repast, when we all went out to dine.

They succeeded in convincing us that they had come in peace
And that our knowledge of the firmament they'd help us to increase.
Some technology they shared,
Then to quickly leave prepared
And promised in the future much more data to release.

A group of sci-fi trekies took the strangers to their heart
And with them on their journey sought permission to depart.
Granted was their fervent plea,
When alien hosts did willingly
Vow to bring them back as they'd found them at the start.

To bid them bon voyage, people came from far and near
And, as the vehicle ascended amidst a massive cheer,
Its rumbling engines shook
And from its gear dislodged a book,
Which became the only evidence to prove that they were here.

Since the book, of course, was printed in a strange and unknown tongue,
To reveal its hidden meaning linguists came from parts far flung.
Naught but title could be read,
Which *"How To Serve Man"* clearly said
And so the praises of these strangers was by all the nations sung.

The world was now convinced we had made a giant leap
And from this brief encounter many benefits would reap.
Celebrations then were planned
To start when they'd return and land.
So filled with joy were people's hearts that they would wildly weep.

But we humans are suspicious, as all by now should know,
And the more we learned about them, the more curious we'd grow.
Were they simply gentle folk,
Or was it to play some eerie joke
That they raced about in spaceships to and fro?

Experts sought by research these mysteries to dispel
And delved into the speechless book to see what it could tell.
Was this the jagged iceberg's tip,
Which 'neath the surface sinks the ship?
Who could know that in deception these travelers would excel?

Scholars worked around the clock with undaunted industry,
Dissecting all known languages, searching for the key.
It was in the conversations,
Which take place between cetaceans,
That the answer was discovered, thanks to creatures of the sea.

When at last the dialecticians deciphered every page,
All the world was quickly thrown into panic, fear and rage,
For this unassuming book
Contained recipes to cook
Earthlings tastefully sautéed with spicy garlic, thyme and sage.

A UFO believer, I was stunned with doubt and fright
And realized at last how we'd been led into this plight.
We had missed the vital clue,
Which placed us in this awful stew,
For are not "*saucers*" known to be their vehicles of flight?

This tale to some, I grant, may seem quite pessimistic,
But when it comes to aliens garbed as altruistic,
Though acting much like friends,
Be cautious of their ends,
Which oftentimes turn out to be morbid and sadistic.

The moral of the story by now should be quite clear.
I'm not suggesting every stranger one must dread and fear,
But with interplanetary gentry,
It may be that "*alimentary*"
More correctly describes the reason they appear.

AUTHOR'S COMMENT: I had watched an episode of the "Twilight Zone," in which a haggard woman was being harassed by what appeared to be tiny human-like creatures, who had entered her house by way of the attic. There was no communication between her and these mysterious intruders and no indication of where they came from until the very end of the show, when the camera focused on a hole in the roof and a tiny spaceship, which had apparently crashed through the roof and bore the glaring and auspicious letters, "NASA." That program captivated my imagination and inspired me to create this piece.

TO LOVE ANOTHER

Which of God's most honored rules
Best governs life's pursuits?
Which provides the vital tools
To harvest its abundant fruit?

Ten delivered on the Mount
Light for us the way.
Telling us the things that count,
They brighten every day.

Among the ten, one stands above;
Alone it will suffice:
"As thyself, thy neighbor love,"
The best of all advice.

The part not often understood
Is the condition that's imposed.
Love of self is truly good,
To which be not opposed.

If indulged in moderation
And carried not to an extreme,
Love of self is no contagion,
But essential self-esteem.

To love another he succeeds,
Whose proper love of self precedes.

LIFE'S ILL-DESIGN

Life is a maze, a series of traps
To catch the traveler unwary,
A journey for which there are simply no maps,
In which each his own baggage must carry.

Around every corner a crisis appears.
A new battle looms for each that is won.
It's filled with excitement, as well as with fears
And chores that just never seem to get done.

How I endure this perpetual fight,
It's beyond me to clearly explain.
At the end of the tunnel, I see a light,
But it's that of an oncoming train.

If God is so kind, all-loving and wise,
Then why this sadistic charade?
Being omniscient, He must recognize
The terrible mess He has made.

If life by mortal men were planned,
Instead of God on high,
Its ill-design I'd understand
And I'd not question, *"Why?"*

Photo by E. G. Pizzella

GOD'S PRECIOUS GEM

Aghast and breathless, struck with awe,
I was stunned by what I saw;
Mountains, valleys, cliffs and bays,
Panoramas that amaze.

Ent'ring Nature's general store,
Wondrous treasures greet the eye.
As one endeavors to explore,
He cannot help but sigh.

Emotions I could not control,
Effervescing, fled my soul,
And, in the words that follow these,
Tell how much those sights did please:

On the seventh day, when God reclined,
I'll wager He did broadly smile,
For perfectly had He designed
His gem, Cape Breton Isle.

AUTHOR'S COMMENT: On August 4, 2001, my companion and I left for a week's vacation in Nova Scotia. We flew Air Canada from Bradley to Montreal and then to Halifax. We spent a couple of days touring Cape Breton Isle and as we drove along the Cabot Trail from Cheticamp to the eastern side of CBI, we were awed by the breathtaking panoramic views to which we were repeatedly exposed. We spent the night at the Inverary Inn in Baddeck. The next morning, we strolled the vast and beautifully landscaped grounds of this luxurious resort. As we passed the tennis courts, we found some inviting lawn chairs on the bank of Lake Bras D'Or. There we settled for a few moments to catch our breath and enjoy the aura of this beautiful lake. Bathed in the glowing warmth of the late morning sun, I grabbed a scrap of paper and scribbled down this poem.

ODE TO WAYWARD SOCKS

When looking for my argyles, I'm subjected to a hosing,
As anxiously I grope within my cluttered drawer.
In utter frustration, I find myself exposing
A mystery none have ever dared explore.

With woven clumps I fumble, fearing I'll be late,
As, in vain, I try to match my socks and dress.
Invariably I'm left with a few that have no mate
And my confusion I'm required to confess.

Endlessly I search, but the culprits can't be found,
As anxiously from room to room I rush.
The more I investigate, the angrier I sound,
Sputtering invectives that would make a sailor blush.

Socks, it seems, like humans, prize their liberty
And in the realm of footwear the divorce rate's clearly flared.
Stockings, once united, now aspire to be free
And have in multitudes rebelled from being paired.

Programs are needed for reconciliation
And on cartons of milk let the wanderers be placed.
No claims of "*podiphilia*" will ever stun the nation,
For their union, though close-knit, is very chaste.

Remarkable, indeed, is this peculiar circumstance,
Where the state of being "*matchless*" is no attribute to boast.
To find a proper mate, quite minute would be the chance,
Even with assistance from yentas coast to coast.

Somewhere there's a place, where wayward socks must go,
In the void of outer space, or in limbo --- who can tell?
There's got to be a place --- I've not seen it, but I know ---
Where a billion unpaired socks in isolation dwell.

Every year I lose a dozen, I'd not hesitate to say,
And I'm just one very average and ordinary guy.
If we assemble like occurrences, near and far away,
We're confronted with a problem that would make a grown man cry.

I envision wily gremlins with at least a thousand feet,
Who lurk in hidden nooks in every home.
Patiently they wait, until we hit the street,
Then voraciously our bureau drawers they comb.

Washers and dryers and hampers do they scour
And hastily they rummage through piles of dirty clothes.
Fully are they cognizant of their inherent power,
Since by their machinations cruelly bared are human toes.

Perhaps it's a plot spawned by those who manufacture
To assure the continuity of their commercial sales.
If so, it's a conspiracy that happily I'll fracture
And I'll bear whatever burden it entails.

A global campaign I declare must now be started
To guaranty that matching socks will nevermore be parted.

AUTHOR'S COMMENT: All my life I have marveled at how frequently matching socks seem to disappear. And it always happens when you're late for an appointment. I became so exasperated with this inexplicable phenomenon that I vented my frustration in the form of poetry.

PERSPECTIVE

"Look again," the teacher said,
"Raise your sights a notch or two.
Change your outlook; tilt your head;
Mount your desk and check the view!"

Life from one position spied
Often tends to be a bore,
But, when a novel viewpoint's tried,
A special thrill's in store.

Do a headstand; try a squint!
Don't get caught in nature's trap,
For life conceals a rosy tint
Beneath its dull and sullen wrap.

As in cooking, add some spice!
Serve life's taste buds with a treat!
Each new discovery's worth the price
Of boredom's guaranteed retreat.

Of every moment make the most
And do what others only dream.
Drive yourself and never coast
And rise above the artless mean.

Perspectives change like night to day,
When life's observed in a different way.

AUTHOR'S COMMENT: I went to see a movie entitled "The Dead Poets' Society" and was so captivated by its theme that this piece resulted.

LIFE'S ALIAS

Heaven's an essential part of each religious creed
And the goal to which the faithful must aspire,
But before an offender may to paradise proceed,
Of sin he must be purged by cleansing fire.

The concept of purgation is sardonically applied
And conjures up a cavern filled with gloom and dank disdain,
Where penitent decedents are routinely purified
And punishment is metered out in pain.

This denigrating den of human castigation
Was in common parlance "*purgatory*" named
And, hailed by theologians as the vessel of salvation,
Has through the years been lauded and acclaimed.

Dante wrote of retribution in dark infernal rings,
Where for their human flaws sinners are enslaved
And there ironically tormented by the very things,
Which most in their mortality selfishly they craved.

Although this dismal depot of temporal consternation
Many have described in intimate detail,
None have yet discovered its precise location
And in their futile search to this very moment fail.

The longer that in patience I endure
This hopeless vale of bitter tears and strife,
The more deeply I'm convinced and feel secure
That purgatory's other name is "*life.*"

Purgatory's function is to restore the soul to worth,
Which process, I believe, occurs right here on earth.

WISDOM IN REFLECTION

"What's the greatest evil of our day?"
Asked a cynic, who clearly was distraught.
It's the violence that terrorists purvey,
Stemming from the hatred they've been taught.

How do we protect our way of life?
How do we continue as before?
Do their atrocities justify the strife
That now propels us headlong into war?

To fail to act is acting none-the-less
And appeasement is a license to destroy.
Toleration simply heightens the distress,
When evil does its tentacles deploy.

The answer's both crystal clear and terse;
To *live* we must put *evil* in reverse!

AUTHOR'S COMMENT: This is another product of the September 11th attack and is a companion to "The Lesson," which appears on page 28.

NINE-ONE-ONE

The eleventh of September
In the year Two Thousand One
Is a date we'll all remember
For the mayhem that was done.

Though the towers may have crumbled,
Causing agony and fear,
That our country's not been humbled
Is a fact that's crystal clear.

Rather than to cow us
And bring us whimpering to our knee,
This horror will endow us
With firm resolve and unity.

It's ironic that the number we would call,
Whenever we might be in need of aid,
Is now instead a date that we recall,
When freedom withstood a frightful raid.

You scoundrels who would liberty assail,
Beware! You've got a tiger by the tail.

Hebron Ave., Glastonbury, CT. Photo by E. G. Pizzella

BEWARE THE I'DS OF MARCH

I'd like to see the snow melt.
I'd like to feel the sun,
The glowing warmth I haven't felt,
Since autumn's course had run.

I'd like to taste what nature yields.
This bulky coat I'd fling.
I'd like to roll in grassy fields
And smell the smells of spring.

I'd like to walk along the shore,
Or climb a lofty peak.
In lush green woodlands I'd explore,
Not to find, but seek.

When winter's chill from earth's sweet bosom's torn,
Behold, the wistful I'ds of March are born.

Photo by E. G. Pizzella

LEMON'S BITTER PILL

To be a hit a polish must be laced with lemon oil
And soaps with lemon scent in popularity are high.
Critical remarks concerning lemons make me boil
And I'd gladly hang those critics out to dry.

I'm a devotee of lemon drops and quenching lemonade.
And is anything more tempting than a tangy lemon pie?
With the sour, perky lemon I'm enamored, I'm afraid,
Except when it's been squirted in my eye.

Lemon zest enhances almost every gourmet dish.
Even lamb chops and spinach sing its praise.
I'm liberal with the lemon juice I sprinkle on my fish
And amazed by all the roles the lemon plays.

On the other hand, I'm crushed when it means a lousy car,
Or a gadget that's defective, a contrivance that's a fraud.
Such terminology's offensive to one who's deemed a star
And by such baseless ridicule I'm absolutely awed.

How could anyone with dignity such slight-of-hand contrive?
Surely to this noble fruit it must be a bitter pill.
This verbal incongruity ought not to survive,
For it's one I'll not accept and never will.

Is its repute not tarnished by the fact its color's linked
To the conduct of cowards, whom we all deplore?
By this frame of reference its armor has been chinked
And the automotive pseudonym ought not to chink it more?

In so callused a manner, why should lemons be demeaned,
When the names of other fruit could as easily be used?
Why have we not on the grapefruit or the lime or orange leaned?
From such denigrating duties why should mangos be excused?

Thoroughly embittered has this citrus fruit become,
Since this ugly misnomer has garnered wide acclaim.
To a sweeter disposition perhaps it might succumb,
If we removed from the vernacular the misuse of its name.

How could language so perversely depict this useful critter?
It's no wonder the lemon became bitter!
Linguistic revision we should advocate with spunk
That the lemon's worthy name may not hence refer to junk.

AUTHOR'S COMMENT: As indicated above, I simply love the taste of lemon – lemon pie, lemonade, lemon juice sprinkled on fish or green vegetables – so I could not tolerate the use of its good name, as a reference to things that are deplorable. My resentment thus inspired me to proclaim my objection to what I considered to be an unpardonable slander.

Photo by E. G. Pizzella

IRONICALLY IRISH

Freedom of speech is a double-edged blade,
Designed for defense, as well as attack.
Wielded with reason progress is made,
But, wielded with malice, it turns progress back.

The Irish in Beantown were anxious to strut
In St. Patrick's Day's annual, festive parade.
Ne'er did they dream that they'd be stuck in a rut,
Or that to court they'd be marching, seeking its aid.

A bevy of gays, when details were revealed,
Claimed a place in that cherished, ethnic event.
To the Federal Court they later appealed,
When their plea was rejected and they homeward were sent.

"Of our right to free speech we've been harshly deprived,"
To a liberal judge they tearfully brooded
And, before the appointed day had arrived,
He ordered that they must, of course, be included.

Abruptly abandoned was the planned celebration,
As the committee itself sought legal redress.
The dispute was resolved with a stark revelation,
Which settled at last a chaotic mess.

The sponsors appealed to a higher court
And sought to reverse the decision below.
To their own legal rights did they staunchly resort,
Which dealt their opponents a shattering blow.

The decision the court handed down was inspired
And put those on the left abruptly in place.
It was not the decree that they had desired,
But the one prescribed by the facts of the case.

It was held that the rights of the sponsors, instead,
By allowing the gay group's officious intrusion,
Would be reckoned for all intents as quite dead,
Killed by their awkward and unwelcomed inclusion.

To its sponsors the fete did surely belong
And its message was theirs to publicly preach.
To alter its meaning would clearly be wrong,
For it was they who would then be deprived of free speech.

To assure that your rights a court will protect,
To the rights of others show proper respect!

AUTHOR'S COMMENT: This poem is based upon an actual Circuit Court of Appeals decision. I fully expected the appellate court to set aside reason and succumb to the current tidal wave of senseless, liberal extremism. If it had done so, this would have been an instance in which the epithet, "the law is an ass," would have indeed applied. I was pleased when the Court instead relied on logic and common sense.

THE DISCOURSE OF THE MUSE

Poetic composition lacks appropriate respect,
For from other skills it clearly stands apart.
While prose is deemed essentially the voice of intellect,
The language of the poet speaks the heart.

Adroitly intermingling the joy of love's caress
With the penetrating sting of lost love's pain,
The poet sketches images that poignantly express
Life's whimsical vicissitudes of which we oft complain.

Within precise parameters he struggles with emotions,
As tediously he works and plies his craft.
He gropes endlessly for words depicting nuances and notions,
Methodically revising each oft rewritten draft.

He bounces like a yo-yo from ecstasy to sorrow,
Tormented by the twist of every phrase,
Hoping revelation, absent now, will come tomorrow
To free him from his self-imposed, confining verbal maze.

Wringing mellow wit from frustration's senseless din,
Yet aware that sound and meter must be prime,
Irresistibly impelled by the spirit trapped within,
He flavors the concoction with precious dabs of rhyme.

He grapples with infinitives, conjunctions and subjunctives,
Striving for pronouncements that ring true.
Carefully he interweaves adverbs and gerundives,
Which, lightly sprinkled, lend their gusto to the brew.

Riding the crest of a flood of inspiration,
Many are the avenues a poet may explore,
As seductively he's lured by frivolous flirtation
With simile, antithesis, hyperbole and metaphor.

"Gestation" best describes the construction of a verse,
As to maturity it grows, springing from a fertile seed.
Its essence can be profiled as pithy, wise and terse,
And both in literature and poet it fulfills a vital need.

And when at last it's finished and the rhythmic work is done,
He pensively reflects and marvels at the thought
That from the same old tired words, with which he'd first begun,
Through poetic ingenuity new beauty has been wrought.

Linguistic insecurity may cause some of us to falter,
While some the art of language may utterly abuse,
But few possess the skill and audacity to alter
The sublime and esoteric discourse of the Muse.

Though poetic definitions for eons have been sought,
Intended to satisfy each literary test,
Poetry, I submit, is "what has oft been thought,"
But, in the eloquence of Pope, "was ne'er so well expressed."

AUTHOR'S COMMENT: My unique experiences in Miss Hoye's English class at Northeast Junior High School during the 1940's aroused my passion for poetry. I remember the flush that came over me when I first read the lyrical poems of Alexander Pope. How can one forget precious nuggets like "A little learning is a dangerous thing?" I was particularly impressed with his classical definition of poetry which inspired and is quoted in this piece.

TOO LATE TO SAY GOODBYE

(Dedicated to those lost in the Alaskan Airline disaster of 02/00.)

With somber brow he sadly knelt
And brushed a tear from neath his eye.
All who observed knew how he felt.
'Twas now too late to say goodbye.

So much more could they have shared.
He cursed the many deeds undone.
Could he have shown how much he cared,
Before the sands of time had run?

With sighs produced by pangs of grief,
Reviled he tender words unsaid.
He found in memories no relief,
For one so loved too soon was dead.

Let idle moments not elapse
Ere love's expression we perfect,
For tearful eulogies and taps
Fill not the void left by neglect.

Photo by E. G. Pizzella

LEGACY OF LUCK

It's been said by those acclaimed for depth of thought
That a teacher by his pupils oft is taught,
Which should, it seems, with equal weight pertain
To those, who similar relationships maintain.

So a lawyer from his clients may on occasion draw
Insights beneficial in dealing with the law.
To me the point was made with clarity and force,
As I embarked with trepidation upon my legal course.

I cite an instance, where I feel one must agree
That I received a great deal more than a monetary fee.
'Twas an event I'm not likely in the future to forget,
Which left me, quite ironically, in my client's debt.

Among my elder clients was a man possessed of wealth,
Whose pale and weak appearance confirmed his failing health.
I proceeded to discuss with him a plan for his estate
And consequently learned he'd been treated well by fate.

I blurted, "You're so lucky," in an off-hand kind of way
And surprised was I, when this remark was greeted with dismay.
"It depends on definition," he retorted with a sneer,
Recalling lengthy hours he'd devoted to career.

"If rewarding one's persistence as luck can be defined,
Then I suppose that life to me has been much more than kind.
But your view is superficial, as with most who envy gain,
For good fortune saves her smile for those, who persevere in pain."

I confess I was embarrassed by what surely was implied,
But gained a bit of wisdom, on which I've since relied,
For he ended the discussion with this clever epithet:
"The harder I work, it seems the luckier I get."

DOUBLESPEAK

I never cease to marvel at how language is abused
By those who seek to justify their deeds.
"Homicide" is *"murder,"* when suspects are accused,
But intending otherwise,
It comes as no surprise
That *"eliminate"* and *"neutralize"*
More clearly state their needs.

This is not to be confused with the parlance of the street,
Where the point is made with force, if not finesse.
No pretense is made in linguistics to compete,
So lacking in good taste
And emphasizing haste,
They *"take out, whack and waste,"*
And graphically conveyed is the message none-the-less.

"Abortion" is a term we're reluctant to apply
And hence we seek a label more appealing.
Innocuous *"pro-choice"* becomes our alibi
And everybody wins,
For we speak no more of sins
Or when precious life begins,
Our true objectives all the while concealing.

In leger-de-main of this linguistic type
Bureaucratic stalwarts take the lead.
Never would they lie, or promote deceit or hype,
But not a moment did they waste
To solve the problem that they faced,
When *"propaganda"* was disgraced.
"Disinformation" was the answer, all agreed.

Since military action is perceived as being cruel,
From *"bombing"* the Air Force must refrain.
Hence the leaders of *"correctness,"* using language as their tool,
Have proposed the introduction
Of a verbal reconstruction
And, in lieu of vile destruction,
What we do instead is *"alter the terrain."*

Military jargon with such examples is replete,
Hence enemy positions will no longer be *"destroyed."*
According to the pros, this lingo's obsolete,
So they've chucked this horrid word
And with modern trends concurred.
Hence *"servicing the target"* is heard
And deemed the proper phrase to be employed.

"Strategic redeployment," which has many liberals awed,
Is a term those on the left will frequently repeat.
To solve the problem in Iraq they've clearly stooped to fraud.
Our national honor they would bend,
As they propose the war to end
And make the enemy our friend,
So what we started would never be complete.

"Drunk" is a label many feel to be offensive
And a substitute thus needs to be contrived.
Intoxication's common, though the habit is expensive,
So to pressure we must yield,
To liberals giving up the field,
As the alternative's revealed.
Voila! A drunk is now *"sobriety deprived."*

When a student flunks his courses, it's forbidden to offend,
So we seek a gentle way to break the news.
To political correctness, though reluctant, we must bend,
For "*failure*" is in disrepute,
A concept we just can't refute.
Thus avoiding what such terms impute,
"*Achieving a deficiency*" saves him from the blues.

When a company's in trouble and expenses it must shrink,
No longer does it callously lay workers off the line.
Sensitive to trends and what the public now may think,
The boss will vacillate and squirm,
But reluctantly confirm
That he must "*downsize*" the firm
To avoid the slightest hint of a decline.

Though the status of the business may have been resolved,
The employee by calamity's been greeted.
The problems that he faces are many and involved
And no matter what we're told,
He's been left out in the cold
And he's probably too old,
So to "*involuntary leisure*" he's retreated.

When the economy has taken a devastating dive
With business failures steeply on the rise
And interest rates have fallen, dropping down from ten to five,
We search for an expression,
Avoiding terms such as "*recession*,"
And arrive at this concession:
"*Disinflation*" more aptly here applies.

The term *"handicapped"* we're cautioned not to use
And "disability" from common talk's removed.
"Crippled" and *"retarded"* are words we dare not choose,
For by prevailing view -
It's both obvious and true -
Such descriptions are taboo,
And *"challenged"* is the term that's now approved.

Those living on the dole require dignity, it's urged,
So titles such as *"welfare"* now are dead.
All denigrating terms from the language must be purged.
To be politically correct
And show parasites respect
These are words we must reject.
Hence *"entitlement"* was chosen in its stead.

Likewise *"poverty"* and *"poor"* remind us of the past.
If you use them, you'll be branded as a rogue.
When we point to the laggards, who as indigents are classed,
To different phrases we must turn
And show the depth of our concern,
Or in hell we'll surely burn.
"Economically oppressed" is now in vogue.

To describe someone as *"fat"* no longer is in style,
For obesity is deemed to be a norm.
Corpulence today is greeted with a smile.
They've got clubs and magazines
Both for seniors and for teens
And, though tents are used for jeans,
"Alternate image" now identifies their form.

Patently it's true that many men are bald
And few from this condition have been spared.
A problem we've encountered is how it should be called
And, though some may hide their crown
'Neath a furry clump of down,
We must be careful not to frown,
As sympathetically we greet the "*follicly impaired.*"

Amazing is the rhetoric one from simple words may pry,
When perversely they're distorted to defend.
In the presidential scandal, "she was never told to lie,"
But there's no question they used spin,
Which made her "cover-story" thin
And cleared the President of sin,
Which proves without a doubt that truth and politics don't blend.

There has thus emerged a game
And "*Doublespeak*" is its name,
Where those of liberal bent
May fuss and fume and vent.
Since truth has taxed their brain
And by clarity they're awed,
They've buckled 'neath the strain
And they're leaning now toward fraud.

Hence eliminating terms that they consider crude,
They've replaced them with phrases of a more complacent mood.
Their pronouncements thus are built
On pillars of enormous guilt
And, curing not life's social ills,
To mountains they've converted hills.
The problem's not the words we say
And with flowery tags won't go away,
But far beneath the surface lies
And painful truth defies.

AUTHOR'S COMMENT: This is my answer to some of the linguistic distortions emanating from and relentlessly foisted upon us by political correctness.

A KNIGHT TO REMEMBER

[Based on the musical play "Man Of LaMancha"]

The greatest story ever told is not what you might think,
But the story of a man, whose mind teetered on the brink.
In bygone days, it's said he roamed LaMancha's barren plain
And his larks, though well intentioned, brought him much disdain.

He'd read vivid tales of chivalry and legends of brave knights
And on their gallant escapades steadfastly set his sights.
Though withered by his many years, he would not be dismayed,
As he donned his makeshift armor and embarked on his crusade.

He vowed to seek out every wrong and every wrong he'd right,
So on his noble steed rode off this avid would-be knight.
Soon he stopped a barber and his shaving basin stole,
Which served him as a helmet in playing out his role.

Encountering a flock of sheep, he went into a trance
And, thinking them an evil hoard, attacked with sword and lance.
For this the shepherds beat him, fighting fire with fire,
And left him in a crumpled heap attended by his squire.

He next attacked a windmill, which seemed an evil giant,
And was brutally repelled in a manner quite defiant.
Weary of their battles, an inn they chanced to see,
Which to this tattered dreamer meant hospitality.

Here he might be dubbed a knight, as in the days of old,
So to prepare his spirit a "vigil" he would hold.
He was led into a courtyard, where he fell upon his knee,
And there was boldly tempted by pompous vanity.

Humbled and ashamed, he confessed and bowed his head.
"Call nothing thine, except thy soul," remorsefully he said
And, fearing that to pride he might reluctantly succumb,
"Love not thy present self, but what thou may become."

There he met Aldonza with manner crude and base
And saw his Dulcinea, an angel in her place.
Through his faith unwavering, she finally became
A lady of high character, befitting that fair name.

Many are the follies that this befuddled knight befell,
Which are skillfully recounted by his author, Don Miguel.
He's frequently described as mad, for reason he defies,
"But, when life itself seems lunatic, who knows where madness lies?

Perhaps to be too practical is madness of a kind,
Or seeking wealth and treasure, where trash is left behind.
To give up dreams may be as mad as too much sanity,
Or seeing life as it is and not as it should be."

The saga of this hapless knight, by which I'm deeply stirred,
Is both profound and bittersweet and yet sometimes absurd.
Some think of Don Quixote as an old and senile clod,
Forgetting that a madman is called "a child of God."

Such are the timeless lessons that this madman's life portrayed.
Would that such a role might by all of us be played.

AUTHOR'S COMMENT: I thoroughly enjoyed playing the role of
Padre Perez in the Hole In The Wall Theatre's production of "Man
Of LaMancha" in New Britain, Connecticut. This was one of HITW's
most successful productions. The show was directed by Justine
Tobis and the music was provided by Ray Shinn at the piano. He
was one of the theatre's founders. When I was first cast in this role,
I read Cervantes' book and became mesmerized by this moving
story and the profound theme, which it shares with the myth of
Pygmalion (see the poem, "The Model Wife" in my collection

entitled "Poetic Myth-Conceptions," soon to be published) and the Broadway musical, "My Fair Lady." I'm convinced that "Man Of LaMancha" is one of the best musical plays ever written and I was captivated by the pithy moral lessons it teaches. Being an avid admirer of Rex Harrison, I was also thrilled with the opportunity to play the role of Henry Higgins in "My Fair Lady," which was produced and directed by Kris McMurray at the Beckley Dinner Theatre in Berlin, Connecticut. For further information on these theatrical productions see my book, "The Versatility Of Chairs."

FALLEN HERO

How ardently we idolized this pinnacle of power,
Who in days of yore impressed this wide-eyed child.
He stood among his peers a bright and shining tower
And, awestruck, we applauded whene'er "the juice ran wild."

His smiling face and manner mild, imprinted on my brain,
Were solid proof this man could do no wrong.
His image on the screen was sunshine in the rain
And strident, raucous din he turned to song.

Calamity's occurred and our hero's caught within.
The evidence of guilt begins to mount.
Is he not untarnished, incorruptible by sin?
Do all his past accomplishments not count?

We tear our inner beings, searching for evasion.
We conjure up excuses. It must have been a frame!
We close our eyes to human flaws that enter the equation
And lead to self-destruction of man as well as name.

Who is this cruel imposter, exposing his humanity?
I cannot, no, I will not believe such horrid things!
I gasp for air! It can't be true! It's sheer insanity!
It's silly how to icons tenaciously one clings.

How can such an idol so feebly tumble down?
From disbelief reluctantly come feelings of betrayal.
Ignominiously the king has forfeited his crown,
In recognition of the fact that man is frail.

Empathy now swells for his tragedy and pain.
His internal wrenching torment stings deeply in our core.
The fantasy is gone and, as our balance we regain,
We see at last the man and nothing more.

Before unbelieving eyes, a hero tripped and fell,
Producing sadness more profound than words can ever tell.

AUTHOR'S COMMENT: O. J. Simpson was my hero. I reveled in his fabulous football career and admired him, as one who truly exemplified the fulfillment of the American dream. When his ex-wife and her companion were brutally slain and it became apparent that he was responsible, I was crushed and dolefully retreated to pen and paper.

Photo by S. J. Miller

THE HOUSE ON QUINTE ISLE

I'm haunted by the house on Quinte Isle
And embedded in my memory is its stare.
Reflective of occult and witches' guile,
It presents to every passerby a dare.

Its gables seem to twist into a scowl,
Warning that intruders have no chance.
Chilling winds whip 'round it with a howl,
As if to threaten any who'd advance.

Its foreboding aura makes the pulse rate rise,
As it wraps itself in shadows like a cape.
Clouds turn menacing before one's very eyes,
As if to thwart a possible escape.

That somber, eerie structure haunts me still
And in distant recollection ever will.

AUTHOR'S COMMENT: Shirley and I enjoyed our many trips to the Millhaven Inn on the northern shore of Lake Ontario in Canada. We would frequently board a ferry and explore the nearby islands, one of which was Quinte Isle. I was captivated by the eerie house depicted above, which appeared to be haunted.

METAMORPHOSES OF SPRING

The stunning metamorphoses of spring
Are occurrences miraculous indeed,
When birds return to nest and gaily sing
And growth appears where none have planted seed.

Gold medallions on a carpet tinted green
May cause a few dissidents to anguish,
Complaining that such weeds their lawns demean,
But to me they are fulfillment of a wish.

Barren trees are festive, decked with flowers.
Frozen brooks, free to babble, are content.
Nature now demonstrates her powers,
As frenzied bees are lured by floral scent.

Nature's annual rebirth is a pleasure to behold,
When everywhere are neophytes and gone are gray and cold.

Photo by E. G. Pizzella

THE LIGHT AT PEGGY'S COVE

Silent, somber and erect,
Standing guard on weathered rock,
Its job to signal and protect,
It plies its craft around the clock.

Stationed on its lofty site,
The tales it harbors would astound,
Of wry Poseidon's awesome might
And vessels cruelly run aground.

Daunted not by gale and storm,
Nature's wrath does it resist,
Enduring bitter cold and warm,
Engulfed in blinding fog and mist.

Relentless vigil it pursues,
Lighting mariners their way,
Providing ships with vital clues
Impending harm to stay.

Aloof with piercing eyes that rove
The vast expanse of restless sea,
The lonely Light at Peggy's Cove
Attests to Man's mortality.

AUTHOR'S COMMENT: This is another of the many captivating scenes we encountered on our enjoyable journeys to Canada and Lake Ontario's north shore.

LEST YE BE JUDGED

[Based on John 8.2 – 11]

Hopelessly abandoned, she cowers in the square,
By her accusers and her perfidy condemned.
Who will render her assistance? Who will even care?
On whom can such a hateful wretch depend?

With narrowed, focused eyes and somber glare,
They silently encircle and enclose,
As stone-filled hands uplifted in the air
Make ready fatal judgment to impose.

At that moment, in their midst there steps a man,
Whose presence halts the murderous charade.
Deliberation and reflection now began
And vengeful stoners were then solemn pillars made.

"Let him among you, who has never sinned,
Be the first to cast the awful telling blow!"
By words so sharply pointed were the executioners pinned,
And in embarrassment they let the woman go.

He offers her his firm and calming hand,
As he gently escorts her from the fray.
Few, who call themselves believers, understand
The true significance of what occurred that day.

His parting words were "Go and sin no more,"
Exposing unequivocally the evil of her deeds.
Condoning not the acts that came before,
The course of her redemption thus he seeds.

Once the sin's committed, its evil must remain,
Yet the doer may be tempted to repent.
Of damage to the rule let none complain,
For this, without a doubt, is what was meant.

"Judge not, lest ye be judged," the man decreed,
Condemning not the doer, but the deed.

AUTHOR'S COMMENT: This is one of the most intriguing examples of Christ's love. But what fascinates me most about this incident is His incredible ability to command without commanding, His ability to employ succinct, demonstrative phrases, which go right to the heart of an issue and demand His desired result, but which are in no way provoking and do not allow for dissent or rebuttal. Another well-known example is the episode in which His enemies sought to trap Him and asked Him if it was appropriate for Jews to pay tribute to Caesar. He simply asked for a coin and, when they presented Him with one, pointing to the Emperor's image on the coin, He said, "Render unto Caesar that which is Caesar's and render unto God that which is God's." How can you argue with that?

WORDS OF LOVE

"I love you! I love you! I love you!"
These words, heard time and time again,
Are twisted by the needs of men.
Employed to justify a fling,
They resonate with hollow ring.

Their use in prolix repetition
Contradicts their definition,
As they abet Man's cheap design.
They are not words of mine!

Words of meaning so profound
Should not be lightly bandied 'round,
But saved for special circumstance,
Profound relations to enhance.

When Man has need of Woman's charms
And warmly holds her in his arms,
He mouths these words to win her favor.
She yields in hope of love to savor
And he repeats them by the score.
Done! And he is seen no more.

Though some may think that I'm confused,
I yet maintain that they're abused.
Such doings should not be excused.
Their frequent use leaves me in awe.
I wish that I could pass a law
To obviate this human flaw.

To Congress I would swiftly race
And ban their use in every case...
Except when I my love embrace.

THE CRITIC

A reviewer's as sour as lemons picked green,
For thought he's enjoyed a show that he's seen,
He'd never admit the actors were good
For fear that his comments might be understood.

Nor would he praise the style of direction,
For every endeavor requires correction.
And what about costumes, props, sets and dance?
He'd never concede that the show they enhance.

The web that he spins must be veiled in mystique,
The ire of his readers to cleverly pique.
Kudos and raves would never suffice
To artfully showcase this pundit's advice.

With candor he boasts of the knowledge he hoards.
To hell with the guys who ply on the boards!
They're just the kids this parent must scold.
Though lacking their talent, he's pompous and bold.

He gleefully points to the flaws he decries,
Proclaiming to all he's theatrically wise.
He often ignores the merits and pluses
To highlight the flubs, which at length he discusses.

And when he's completed his lethal incision,
He expects all his readers to reach one decision;
Not about theatre, to laud or to blame,
But just that this "critic" has earned his good name.

AUTHOR'S COMMENT: In 1990, I was cast as Horace Vandergelder
in Southington Community Theatre's production of "Hello Dolly,"

which was directed by Tom Chute. I was pleased to meet and work with Joyce Follo of Southington, who was brilliant in the role of Dolly Levi. After the opening night performance, the cast waited with bated breath for the Southington Observer's review. Although it complimented the leading actors, it was mercilessly critical of all other aspects of the show. I felt that the review was unfair and thus attacked the critic with my pen.

Photo by E. G. Pizzella

SEDUCED BY SEDONA

Crimson cliffs and ruddy ridges,
Perched on red rock pillars high,
Probe with spiny spires and ledges,
Threatening puffy clouds and sky.

Rosy tinted, stone-faced giants,
Poised and guarding vales of sand,
Exhibit grim and grave defiance
And staunch against intrusion stand.

Crusty crests with cloudy crowns
That rise from mounds besmirched with green,
Warn travelers from their distant towns
That they'll view sights they've never seen.

Jagged crags with snowy peaks
And canyons streaked with red and gray
Provide the seeker all he seeks,
As nature spreads its vast array.

Among the charms of Arizona,
The most seductive is Sedona.

AUTHOR'S COMMENT: When we were fortunate enough to visit and travel in Sedona, we were truly mystified and seduced by its scenic marvels, which loomed before us everywhere we went. It seemed like we were tiny insects, roaming around in the play-yard of an energetic and imaginative child, frantically building sand castles.

THE FOX AND THE CROW

[Based on "Le Corbeau Et Le Renard" by Jean De La Fontaine]

Perched high in a tree, a crow sought repose,
As he held in his beak a stout wedge of cheese.
A fox, who was lured by its smell in his nose,
Thus addressed him with comments like these:

"Good morning my friend, Mister Crow!
I'm impressed by your radiant glow!
In truth I must say, if your tones to my ear
Are as pleasing as you to my eyes now appear,
The envy of all indeed you must be,
Who reside in this rural vicinity.

The gullible bird, bloated with pride,
His mellifluous voice no longer could hide
And opened his beak, thus releasing his treasure,
Which the fox quickly seized with the greatest of pleasure.

"What's occurred here," said he, "demands that we learn
A rule which to all greatly matters.
Him, who lavishes praise, one must spurn,
For he feeds on the one whom he flatters."

The crow's foolish vanity thus was displayed
And the lesson he learned was worth what he paid.
In the end, overwhelmed by guilt and confused,
He swore that he'd never again be so used.

AUTHOR'S COMMENT: Here again, as in "Impressions Of My Lady," "The Ant And The Grasshopper" and "Prologue To Eternity," I have taken a poem written in another language and not only translated it, but I have cast the translation in poetic form. I find this literary exercise truly exhilarating. Another example of this can be found on page 122, "The Ant And The Grasshopper."

GENDER YAP

Like revenuers after farmers' stills,
Incessantly they harp on gender ills.
The system each assails
Is a *"System run by males*;
Society is sick and needs some pills."

Male chauvinists now recognize their plight.
"To keep the status quo by God we'll fight!
To the language that we own,
Not one change will we condone.
Male superiority's a blessing, not a blight."

But think of how they've clarified our tongue.
Feministic praises ought loudly to be sung.
"Mailmen" now are dead,
Replaced by *"carriers"* instead,
Dispelling any clouds which o'er that title hung.

What function did the former *"mailman"* serve?
Why must ambiguity be something we preserve?
Did he deliver or receive?
'Twas intended to deceive,
But now the function from the title we can readily observe.

"Firemen" have undergone the same linguistic fate.
Is a conflagration something they extinguish or create?
As to their job, there's now no doubt.
A *"fighter"* puts the fire out,
Thus eliminating need for discussion and debate.

With reluctance, the Teamsters now must disaffirm
What's reputed to have made the union movement firm.
Despite its former high position,
Its use is presently sedition,
For *"boycott"* has become an anachronistic term.

For "manhole" and "mannequin," it's apparently too late,
And we mourn the loss of "mandible" and "manipulate."
It's impossible to know
Just how far we'll have to go
To implement what seems an unattainable "mandate."

Never more will a "policeman" pound a beat.
To become an "officer" the ladies now compete,
And lest you think it's all bologna,
Men bring suits for alimony
And sexist terms like "housewife" are doomed as obsolete.

Linguistic alteration reduces sexual strife.
Political correctness is now a way of life.
Sensitivity's the cause
And it merits our applause.
She's called "domestic partner," not a wife.

Substance on occasion may result from an extreme,
For things are not what on the surface they may seem.
We should not regard as strange
That language must keep up with change
And importance must be placed on self-esteem.

THE ANT AND THE GRASSHOPPER

[Based on "La Cigale Et La Fourmi" by Jean de la Fontaine]

Having sung all summer long,
The grasshopper still chirped her song,
'Til winter's chill at last came 'round
And she an empty cupboard found.

Straight to her neighbor, Mrs. Ant,
She hastened with a plaintive chant.
"Lend me some grain," became her plea,
"And summer next, I guarantee
That I'll repay whate'er was lent
With interest. You'll get every cent."

Now Mrs. Ant few faults did own,
Save one, that she denied the loan
And, doing so, these queries posed:
"Did you not chant while others strained?
By guilt are you not somewhat pained?
Since singing earned you not a sou,
Try dancing! See what that will do."
And thus her foolishness exposed.

The lesson from this poignant tale
None with reason can assail,
That he who fritters time away
With deprivation soon will pay.

AUTHOR'S COMMENT: Another translation of Jean de la Fontaine's poems, "The Fox And The Crow," can be found on page 119.

Photo by E. G. Pizzella

THE PRINCE OF ISLES

Have you ever spent an August eve
At this island's balmy shore,
Where the cool sea breeze
Drifts forth with ease,
Weary travelers to restore?

Have you ever viewed red sandstone cliffs
That hold the sea at bay,
As they guard the yields
Of abundant fields
With their scattered rolls of hay?

Have you ever sniffed the fragrant scent
Of the wild and thorny rose,
Which in rocky turf,
Near sand and surf,
Proliferates and grows?

Have you ever met such gentle folk,
Devoid of ruse and guile,
Who to a high degree
And indeed with harmony,
Do varied cultures blend with utmost style?

Have you ever seen the summer sun
Slowly sink at the Southwest Light,
Where violet hues
And vivid blues
Kiss the Prince of Isles goodnight?

Recalling these prized impressions,
I cannot help but smile,
For they top the list
Of what I've missed,
Since I left Prince Edward Isle.

AUTHOR'S COMMENT: We thoroughly enjoyed our travels in Nova Scotia and on Prince Edward Isle. See the poem entitled "The Captain On The Bridge" at page 274, which focuses on the statue of a sea captain at the foot of the bridge, which connects Prince Edward Isle to the mainland.

SOUR GRAPES

[Based on St. Matthew 20.1-16]

The owner of a vineyard emerged therefrom one day
In search of able workers to harvest ripened fruit.
To those employed in early morn he offered one day's pay
And accepted was this offer by each diligent recruit.

Three hours elapsed and more workers were hired,
To whom it was promised their pay would be just.
Again time elapsed and more help was required,
Who then were engaged on the terms just discussed.

In the evening the owner's goodwill was displayed,
As he ordered the wages to now be disbursed.
Those employed first were the last to be paid,
While those hired later were settled with first.

The wage paid to each was exactly the same,
A full day's pay though some started late.
The last to be paid did loudly complain,
Demanding payment at a much higher rate.

"Weren't you paid what you asked?" inquired the boss.
"Then how can you say that you've suffered a loss?
And may I not pay others more than I owe?
Curtail your greed! Take your earnings and go!"

AUTHOR'S COMMENT: When this story is told today, the knee-jerk
reaction of most people will be that the vineyard owner was unfair
to those, who had worked the entire day. But how can the faithful
performance of a reasonable and voluntary, bilateral agreement be
characterized as "unfair?" Most folks today have been indoctrinated
with the labor union fixation that everyone must be treated equally

without reference to the factual context. Yet it is the factual context that must first be examined in order to determine the rights of the parties. If one objectively considers the facts in this narrative, there can be no question that the vineyard owner acted with integrity. This parable was designed to expose the surreptitious evil of envy. With the application of reason and logic it must be concluded that the vineyard owner was honorable and that those first hired were consumed with greed. This parable is undoubtedly the source of the oft heard expression for unfounded indignation, "sour grapes."

Photo by E. G. Pizzella

THAT'S CATS

Felines are inscrutable, a truly mystic breed,
A peculiar sort of furry household pet.
They're creatures we adopt and house and feed,
But from whom there's very little that we get.

Though we give them our love and endless caring,
Our requests for attention they ignore.
They appear to be demeaned by thoughts of sharing
And our proximity seems to be a bore.

They stare at us at times like we're insane.
They're detached and haughty and demure.
Supreme within their little worlds they reign,
Where humans are a notch above manure.

After eons of abuse, I smell a rat
And the revelation sends me through the roof,
For what I've always thought to be a cat,
I'm now amazed to find is just aloof.

AUTHOR'S COMMENT: Above is a photo of Simpson, our red tabby, who died several years ago at age 20. He was incredibly bright. See the comment following "My Laptop" at page 224.

WORD POWER

In my youth, by the power of language stirred,
I recited with vim and with zeal,
Giving dimension to each vital word
With a rapture I could not conceal.

Throughout my existence, I've nurtured this knack,
Playing games with linguistic expression.
Words are the cannon that mount my attack
And my olive branch of concession.

Words are my solace in fits of dispair,
My vent when anger arises,
My missives of love to say that I care,
My escape in poetic disguises.

Words are the tools of mechanics of verse,
The bricks with which history is built,
Invectives used to condemn and to curse,
The threads of our cultural quilt.

The function of words, most plainly revealed,
Is to convey the thoughts in one's mind.
Without them ideas would there be concealed
And to knowledge all would be blind.

Words entertain; by them empathy's wrought.
They lift up the spirit, yet conjure up fears.
They're frequently sold, borrowed and bought,
Moving listeners to laughter, as well as to tears.

Words form the marrow of order and law,
Of every pursuit, every plan.
Embellished and polished, or simply served raw,
From the beast they separate Man.

Imagine the chaos and utter distress
In a world without words and all they express!

Photo by E. G. Pizzella

A TRIBUTE TO SAN ANTONIO

An odd and ruddy tower looms above the flat terrain,
Not far from where the hallowed fortress stands.
Its futuristic form moves purists to complain,
Those who lack the insight that moves the artist's hands.

Designed by Sebastian, as the city's invitation,
The tangled Torch of Friendship irreverently stands tall.
A symbol quite unique among the cities of the nation,
It graciously extends its hospitality to all.

Some consider it incongruous, while others fawn with praise,
As it highlights San Antonio at history's cultural divide.
Combining to entrap us in a captivating maze,
Here old and new traditions gently flourish side by side.

My trip across the country was complete,
When on the lovely River Walk I placed my wandering feet.

PROFESSIONAL PRIDE

Debating the history of their respective fields,
They argue back and forth throughout the night.
The lively discussion heightens and reveals
The all-consuming passion that drives the endless fight.

The attorney, the doctor and the crafty engineer,
Each was thoroughly convinced that he was right.
Not one of them harbored a scintilla of fear,
But each mounted his attack armed with history's awesome might.

"Mine's the oldest!" said the surgeon. "Can there be a doubt?
Eve was made from Adam's rib. Do you not recall?"
This induced the advocate and engineer to pout,
As they pondered how defeat they might forestall.

Taking the floor with a glimmer in his eye,
The engineer with confidence began his recitation:
"Did the Lord not from chaos make the heavens and the sky
And in six short days complete the earth's creation?

This clearly was the first great engineering feat,
Which thus makes my vocation the senior of the three."
'Twas the counselor and physician, who stared now at defeat,
For with this obvious conclusion, who could disagree?

But the lawyer, filled with pride, refused to be outdone
And simply pointed out how chaos was begun.

FLAW AND ORDER

"Those bleeding hearts will empty out our jails,"
Old-timers with vehemence assure.
That admonition to this day prevails
And draws me to the right, where I'm secure.

I was startled by a case in New York City,
Where a killer was allowed to roam at large,
Since his attorney, impervious to pity,
Impressed a liberal judge who was in charge.

A bloodstained knife, retrieved beneath a bench
In a public park the murderer called home,
Produced the most offensive legal stench
And thus the futile whine voiced by this poem.

That the blood was proved the victim's there's no doubt,
Nor that the fingerprints matched those of the accused.
Such damning evidence was nonetheless thrown out,
That the defendant's precious rights be not abused.

Since the slayer had no home, like you and me,
A legal fiction by his honor was imposed.
"The bench," he ruled, "was his abode, you see,
And, without a warrant, its fictitious door was closed."

A similar occurrence in the Nutmeg State arose,
Involving one who 'neath a bridge resided.
Though condemned by his hidden, blood drenched clothes,
He was released because a liberal judge presided.

Evidence of guilt has routinely been excluded,
Where life's pleasures by a felon have been missed.
The ends of justice are thus cleverly eluded
By invoking rights that simply don't exist.

Substituting guilt forms the base of liberal thought,
Making crime the wilted fruit of plants deprived.
Responsibility is shifted from offender who's been caught
And to society the blame is then ascribed.

The exclusionary rule, although it was designed
To protect us from unauthorized intrusion,
By a liberal justice system has now been redefined
To thwart legitimate attempts at prosecution.

In defense of those who boldly break the law,
Is not excessive zeal a fatal flaw?

AUTHOR'S COMMENT: This poem represents the combined product of my conservative bent, as well as my growing distaste for the deplorable leftward course of our judicial system. The first expression of that distaste emerged in "Legal Aspects." Similar eruptions were subsequently spewed in the form of "A Lawyer's Lament" and "A Legal Opinion." When I wrote "Flaw And Order," I had previously read about the New York decision and was utterly shocked. The guilt of the accused was not a matter of suspicion. It was not a hunch. There was absolutely no question of his culpability in the perpetration of the most heinous crime and yet he was dispassionately released on a technicality. If this were simply the unavoidable consequence of applying the traditional prohibition against illegal search and seizure, the result, though repugnant, might still be palatable. But this was not a traditional application of the exclusionary rule. There was no intrusion. There was no violation of the accused's right to privacy, because the murder weapon was found in a public park. The travesty occurred when the liberal judge, apparently motivated by some perverted sense of societal guilt, totally disregarded reality and converted a bench in a public park into a fictional "home." How could the investigating officer have ever imagined that such a bizarre limitation would be placed upon his investigatory efforts? Insult was added to injury when, in a comparable situation, a Connecticut court relied upon the New York case as precedent. In the Connecticut case, the murderer lived under a bridge abutment, where the excluded evidence was found. When I became aware of these absurd liberal distortions, I was infuriated and voila!

THE RULE OF DE MINIMUS

When first I studied law, I came across a basic rule;
"De minimus non curat lex," is what I learned.
Being rusty in my Latin, I felt somewhat like a fool,
For I thought with minors' rights it was concerned.

Illusions that prevail about the law I'll now dispel,
For I've mastered that motto's true intent.
I've concluded that this rule above all others should excel,
For on trivia too much time the courts have spent.

Is the Pledge of Allegiance tainted by its mention of God?
Can a child sue his parents because they are poor?
Courts employ many fictions that historically are odd
And to frivolity have now unlocked the door.

Big tobacco is sued for smokers' ills
And those who make the guns, when shots are heard.
McDonald's is sued for patron's spills.
When will we dispense with the absurd?

The rule of *de minimus* courts should strictly invoke,
That justice may not seem a silly joke.

Photo by E. G. Pizzella

AUTUMN LEAVES

Golden blotches everywhere,
But not a nugget for my purse,
Nor a bright doubloon to spare,
To make the matter worse.

Scarlet stains a world of green,
Causing fears to rise.
When not a drop of blood is seen,
Observers vent their sighs.

Yellow, orange, rust, maroon
Complete the motley fall array,
But calloused winds are coming soon
To wisk them all away.

CANINE DESIGN

How can one define
A creature so robust?
Erratic, yet sublime,
And always filled with trust.

Selfless love that's pure
With needs to be fulfilled;
Impatient, to be sure,
But by your presence thrilled.

What is it that you see
When you look into those eyes?
A world that's trouble free,
Devoid of any guise.

Wont never to seditiously offend,
No wonder he's been called a man's best friend.

CHAIRS

In all my days I've never viewed
A thing so bountifully imbued,
As that on which I sit my seat,
Whose praises I shall now repeat.

Most humble of all furnishings,
Hard of surface or with springs,
Chairs are found where folks recline,
At home, at work and where they dine.

As though by Nightingale inspired,
Supporting those infirm or tired,
Who, other than a lowly chair,
Exhibits such concern and care?

Though often blank in their expression,
Chairs, too, are subject to depression,
For, like us folks, who troubles share,
Weighty burdens do they bear.

They neither court, nor do they marry
And, though their life is sedentary,
For themselves they've made a niche;
Beloved are they by poor and rich.

I've found, if chairs are not abused,
With loyalty they seem infused,
And this is why they've gained renown,
As never prone to let one down.

No bias do they e'er display,
Embracing all who come their way,
And, though they hold us up at times,
They've ne'er committed any crimes.

Their sheer simplicity beguiles,
But having walked for several miles,
The traveler's pleased to find a chair,
To which he hastens to repair.

I'd buy their stock without delay,
For chairs, I'll vow, are here to stay.
Invulnerable to changing trends,
They neatly gather up loose ends.

Of plastic, metal or of wood,
A chair has in its life withstood
A sum of weight one cannot measure,
Sedately bearing loads at leisure.

Chairs cater not to folks high born,
But offer solace to those forlorn.
Though they may be devoid of wit,
On them both weak and mighty sit.

The functions of a chair are clear
And it performs them without peer.
So let us not be condescending,
For its job is one that's never ending.

The beans I'm here inclined to spill,
For though it does its work with skill,
In its endeavors, bear in mind,
It will often get behind.

Enticing though the baker's trade,
In view of all the dough he's made,
If shapely buns should pull your chain,
Imagine all that chairs contain.

Appearing passive and inert,
A chair wields power to assert,
For, lacking inspirational gifts,
It yet persistently uplifts.

It's something every king must own,
Though in this context it's a throne;
And college management it shares,
For aren't department heads called chairs?

In corporations, thank the Lord,
It's the CEO, who chairs the Board.
So you see they're not just common grunts,
But capable of many stunts.

No object surely can compare
In breadth of usage to a chair,
Whose sturdy limbs are firmly set
To hold a person, thing or pet.

A ladder, stool or table top;
Its applications never stop.
They're obvious to every eye,
Yet there are more some do not spy.

Evading not the grueling chore,
With vigor did I then explore
And thus with confidence opine
A chair exceeds its plain design.

To most a chair is just a seat,
But there are others you will meet
To whom a chair may represent
Each item in the firmament.

A theatre buff is one of these.
A chair is everything he sees.
Rehearsals start; the stage is bare,
So every set piece is a chair.

A chair's a window, couch or door,
A wall or stairs and even more;
A place or thing of every kind,
Whatever's in the playwright's mind.

While other things are incidental,
In theatre chairs are fundamental.
With varied ids in its collection,
It never fails to take direction.

Unrestrained, unfettered, free,
A chair evokes diversity.
It whisks us off upon a trip,
Impersonating train or ship.

A vehicle it well could be;
Accouterments of royalty;
Antiques; equipment used in sport;
Contrivances of any sort.

No limits is it bound to heed
And therefore meets our every need.
Never ceasing to amaze,
One marvels at the roles it plays.

In this vain a chair will test
The skills with which an actor's blessed,
His discipline and concentration
And, most of all, imagination.

AUTHOR'S COMMENT: This poem is closely related to the book I published in 2014 entitled, "The Versatility Of Chairs," which is a theatrical memoir. I was active in community theatre for some thirty-six years and played major roles in more than one hundred productions. I also produced and directed a number of shows. My first venture on stage was in a comedy role, as a stand-in for an actor who had had a dispute with the director and walked out several days before opening. Because I had come in at the last minute, I was not familiar with the six to eight week rehearsal process that preceded opening night. In my next show, in which I played a leading role, I began to recognize the significance of chairs in the rehearsal process. When rehearsals begin, there is no set, so set pieces are represented by chairs, i.e. a chair can represent a table, a sofa, a door etc. This revelation inspired me to write the poem and thereafter to refer to this theatrical trick in the title to my book.

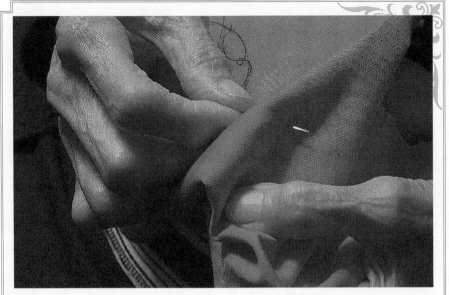

Photo by Shu

NONNI'S LOVING HANDS

Hands that nurtured children with love and selfless care,
Conferring constant sustenance with energy to spare;
Hands that protected and sheltered us from harm
And offered us safe harbor, quelling our alarm;
Hands that taught the lessons of life's complicated scheme;
Hands that always lifted and never would demean;
Hands that welcomed strangers and opened every door;
Hands that encouraged us, our talents to explore;
Hands endowed with industry and optimistic zeal,
Furnishing support and helping ailments heal;
Hands that were extended to help in every need
And, clasped, were upward pointed, asking God to intercede;
Hands that knew no limit of kindness to bestow,
That touched the hearts of all, the seeds of love to sow;
Hands providing comfort, despite obstacles and pain;
Hands that always gave and never sought to gain;
Hands that shunned dissension and always sought accord;
These were Nonni's hands. They now assist the Lord.

AUTHOR'S COMMENT: My mother died in 2010, at the age of ninety-eight. She was the most wonderful woman I have ever known and my mentor. She was my motivation for all that I have accomplished during my lifetime and I adored her. She was also a wonderful seamstress. Shirley, my companion, is a marvelous photographer and one day decided to take a photo of my mother's hands while she was sewing. After she passed on, I again looked at that picture and was inspired to craft this eulogy.

Photo by E. G. Pizzella

DAVID'S DEBUT

I marveled at the skill with which the stone was hewn,
The vital, subtle symmetry of each penetrating stroke.
The sculptor to posterity has bequeathed a gracious boon,
Which will for all eternity excessive awe evoke.

An admirer, it's said, approached the artist and inquired:
"From the moment you began, had you ever any doubt?"
The craftsman's glib response, though casual, was inspired:
"When first I tapped the block of stone, he simply wandered out."

And there he's proudly posed for generations,
With rapture filling all who come to view,
Knowing well that his miraculous creation
From sheer genius did fortuitously ensue.

Hidden since the start of time within that massive block,
Unaware of his surroundings and the ticking of the clock,
David from his catatonic doze at length awoke,
Jostled by the tapping of the chisel's rhythmic stroke.

'Tis a truth, which from days of yore is by every sculptor known:
The work of art in final form resides within the stone.

COMMENTARY: I was attending mass one Sunday morning, when the celebrant in his sermon told the story about Michelangelo and the David. A viewer asked the sculptor how he was able to craft such a perfect form. The artist replied that, as soon as he looked at the block of stone and started tapping on his chisel, David just walked out. From that fertile seed sprang "David's Debut." And I was fortunate to experience the thrill of viewing that incomparable work of art, when in 2009 I traveled with my daughter, Laura, and her family to Italy and viewed it at arm's length.

Photo by E. G. Pizzella

THE FLIGHT OF THE BUMBLEBEE

The virtue of positive thinking
Should never be overlooked,
For it can save a vessel from sinking,
Or one's goose from ending up cooked.

An example deserving applause
Is the corpulent bumblebee,
Who defies all the physical laws
To flutter unfettered and free.

His aerodynamic design
Engineers would term a disaster,
Yet his efforts, one must opine,
Make pollination much faster.

He flits from flower to flower
And flaunts his voluminous size,
Which proves aeronautical power
From ego alone can arise.

The restraints which shorten our stride
Are those which spring from inside.

AUTHOR'S COMMENT: I had attended my grandson, Aaron's graduation from eighth grade. In his remarks to the graduates, the Principal emphasized the importance of striving to attain goals and admonished them not to be deterred by self-imposed limitations. He used the analogy of the bumblebee who, despite his awkward configuration, is yet agile in flight and performs tasks essential to our very existence. I could not resist the temptation to express this analogy in poetic form.

THE FUNCTIONS
OF THE HEART

Why do people say that love is spawned within the heart?
Couldn't this emotion bloom in some other body part?
Now I ask you, "Would it matter
If its home were in the bladder?"
How did this moronic misconception start?

Symbolic of affection in each context and degree,
This bulbous protuberance is a total mystery.
Its artistic depiction
Is a fraud, deceit and fiction,
For it resembles not at all what doctors see.

Why this oddly shaped enigma as the emblem of romance,
When there are many other parts that deserve an equal chance?
As though by edict from above,
It's the source of human love.
Can't any other structure to such prominence advance?

Why hail this mass of muscle as love's principal domain?
Would it not be more appropriate to love with all one's brain?
Or maybe with the stomach or the spleen?
The skeptics are aware of what I mean,
But am I the only brazen fool who's ever dared complain?

If love's conception in the pancreas, one were to propose,
To what pernicious plight would we our partners thus expose?
There are some who truly feel
That we could even use the heel,
But then would jilted lovers have to walk upon their toes?

Love's said to be the force that makes this planet spin,
Which gives you some idea of the predicament we're in.
Unless my guess I've missed,
Its image needs a twist,
So let's proclaim its source to be the tibia or the shin.

Couldn't this sensation find repose within the spine?
The liver or appendix or the lungs would do just fine.
Perhaps duodenum or back,
Or some swollen gland or sack?
How did such a shapeless blob to this seat of power climb?

How about the kidney? That's a nook we might select.
As an organ it's well known and has surely gained respect.
Would it then be truly spoken
That his kidney had been broken,
When one's amorous advances, his lover might reject?

I admit that on occasion I've embarked upon a frolic,
And my heart's been caused to palpitate by the presence of a trollop.
Is this the reason it's so dubbed,
While other parts are coldly snubbed?
The focal point of love should be the collarbone or polyp.

How can we escape the heart's profound hypnotic spell?
Other protoplasmic lumps I'm sure could serve as well.
For instance, one of those
Might even be the nose,
If only we could teach some other organ how to smell.

Can we assume that love's mystique would indefinitely linger,
If we should designate its place of birth to be within the finger?
Or we might instead promote
The tonsils or the throat,
But then would love's crescendo be reserved for naught but singer?

If love's gestation in the ankle, I were boldly to suggest,
Would this not give our pectoral pump a badly needed rest?
If it's doubtful this would fly,
Then I commend the ribs or thigh.
It's surely difficult to find the body part that's best.

Why does this foolish fallacy enjoy such broad appeal?
Have we to fantasy surrendered in the heat of boundless zeal?
But if this function's reassigned,
It stands to reason we must find
An organ which with romance can more dispassionately deal.

A place of wide renown is what we presently must seek.
Would double chin or clavicle be cloisters too unique?
Or we could nominate the buttocks or the hips,
Or enlist the aid of bones or ruby lips.
Lord! The prospect of consensus seems so bleak.

Options so numerous with ease could make one numb,
As to futile indecision we reluctantly succumb.
Why become a total wreck?
Just appoint the head or neck,
Or settle with reluctance for a temple, vein or thumb.

Why have we historically so circumscribed our view,
When there are other courses we could easily pursue?
The thyroid or the colon or the ear
Would be among the first to volunteer.
This needed change in custom I contend is overdue.

If exposure of this sham I should solemnly espouse,
Whose righteous indignation would such a goal arouse?
If it were deemed in proper taste
For one to love with all his waist,
Then those of large dimension could politely take their bows.

In the transfer of this function I'd most certainly delight,
If transition could occur without engaging in a fight.
It would come as no surprise,
If selected were the eyes,
But then the adage "Love is blind" we'd be required to rewrite.

There still remain the arteries, the armpits and the skin,
But however hard we try, it seems doubtful that we'll win.
Tradition is so strong
That we fail to see what's wrong,
Which leads directly to the quagmire that we're in.

Perhaps this trap that binds us could somehow be unsprung,
If within an ample cheek love's burden could be flung?
This would surely be a joke,
For we'd pucker when we spoke,
And where the devil would we henceforth lodge the tongue?

I've embarked upon a mission to destroy this childish myth,
But I'm frankly at a loss for a part to do it with.
So many have been tried,
Yet success has been denied,
Though we've delved into the quandary's very pith.

I predict this revolution will triumphantly succeed.
A single-minded devotee of love is what we need.
Now what would be the harm
Of using shoulder, wrist or arm?
And from this painful chore the heart would then be freed.

The job of pumping blood should be its sole concern.
Will those of us who have one this lesson ever learn?
It's no wonder that they break.
How much pressure can they take?
Amorous pursuits are what a prudent heart should spurn.

It's an anatomic problem I'll just never understand.
Why not love with all one's elbow, foot or hand?
Or with the pelvis or the knee?
I think most folks would agree
That the functions of the heart were poorly planned.

AUTHOR'S COMMENT: One Valentine's Day, as I was shopping for cards appropriate to the occasion, I focused on the beautifully symmetrical heart symbol everywhere displayed to denote emotions of an amorous nature. It hit me like a bolt of lightening. I was familiar with human anatomy. "That doesn't look like a heart," I said to myself. And that's when I began to wonder why love has always been so closely associated with that particular human organ. So much so that it is now frequently used as a symbolic abbreviation in text. Voila! I began to write and I couldn't stop. I think I've counted as many as 55 body parts in this poem.

IF THERE'S A STAGE

[Dedicated to the fond memory of Harry "Al" Barron of Southington]

Who is this man I felt I knew?
What made him dear to me?
This type of person's all too few,
Which now is clear to me.

He loved his family, one and all.
To him their place was number one.
But next he loved a curtain call.
Performing was his fun.

A dozen years ago we met,
Auditioning for a show.
He had a vim I'll not forget,
A radiant theatre glow.

A wide-eyed cherub filled with awe
Surrendered to his yearning.
He noted all he heard and saw,
Eager to be learning.

In "Radio Hour" he played old Pops.
His Applegate was quite a treat.
He coyly pulled out all the stops,
As Kipplinger in "Plaza Suite."

He thus began his stage career
Disclosing great ability,
But we who knew him had no fear
That he'd lose his humility.

In "Dracula" the English Doc;
In "My Fair Lady," Pickering;
His Melvin Thorpe fit like a sock.
Adeptly did he sing.

In "Sugar Babies" he was drole,
Though sometimes backstage he might doze.
Every time he took a role
A new character arose.

He loved to make an audience laugh.
He loved to hear applause.
He earned respect from crew and staff.
Perfection was his cause.

He was a pleasure to direct,
Because he truly loved his art,
Which he sought always to perfect,
Though large or small the part.

We worked together as a team
In "Opal" and in "Outward Bound."
The hours spent like minutes seem
And the time devoted would astound.

"The Odd Couple," our pride and joy,
Was several times repeated.
Complaining of the smoke was Roy,
Who claimed that Oscar cheated.

I felt secure with him on stage.
I knew he always had his line.
We memorized page after page
And he had faith that I had mine.

Of each achievement he was proud.
His family came to each event.
His gait was sure; his voice was loud
And he relished every moment spent.

Theatre quenched his avid thirst
And on the stage he had few peers.
His crowning jewel was "Who's On First,"
A joy we shared for years.

Through every trial he kept his cool.
He learned the rules and lived them well.
Though on the stage he played the fool,
In life and art did he excel.

This chapter's written, so turn the page.
We'll surely miss him, we who care,
But if in heaven there's a stage,
You can bet that he'll be there.

AUTHOR'S COMMENT: Al Barron of Southington occupied a special place in my theatrical world. His interest in theatre did not germinate until middle age. We were holding auditions for a comedy at our banquet facility, L'Auberge d'Elegance on Route 6 in Bristol, Connecticut. I was surprised to witness this middle aged man, who had never been on stage, auditioning for a minor role. He was exceptionally eager and I was impressed by his fervor and commitment. He learned quickly and soon became a very competent actor. We thereafter shared many wonderful experiences in our theatrical activities.

VITAL VITTLES

"What's the food of life," you ask?
"What nurtures us for life's travails?
Can it be found in box or flask,
Or canisters or pails?"

Life's a banquet, I assure you,
Replete with every tempting dish.
Candied hopes and smiles will lure you.
What need is there for meat or fish?

Before each hungry soul it's spread.
You'd think that folks would die to taste it.
But few are those whom it has fed.
On multitudes it's wasted.

This fabled feast to all exposes
Delicious treats that satiate,
Seducing eyes and tongues and noses,
And causing guests to salivate.

A potpourri of promises,
Their prompt fulfillment realized;
Quiches crammed with hugs and kisses;
Fidelity that's caramelized;

Naughty notions by the scoop;
Ambitions lightly toasted;
Ripe reflections stirred in soup;
Inventive genius roasted;

A salad of nostalgic greens;
Puddings spiced with precious time;
Bowls of bright bucolic scenes;
Tarts of lilting song and rhyme;

Omelets drenched with melted dreams;
Entertainments diced and grilled;
Pastas tossed with saucy themes
And crepes with inspirations filled;

A thick fondue of reveries;
Cuddles wrapped within a bun;
Steaming pots of pleasantries;
Tangy fricassees of fun;

Hors d'oeuvres of crisp, creative thought;
Aspirations flaked and browned;
Infectious humor freshly caught,
Baked in fritters, plump and round;

A smorgasbord of flattery
With gentle denigrations;
Canapés of empathy
With drizzled expectations;

Nestled in exotic urns
Simmer sultry passions;
Casseroles of deep concerns,
Sprinkled with attractions;

A succotash of salutations,
Garnished with glad, gaping grins;
Shelled and pickled stimulation's,
Smartly packed in cookie tins;

Jellied joys in crystal crocks,
Topped with adulation;
Whispers crackling on the rocks
With twists of admiration;

Pates of peppered platitudes;
A consommé of charm;
Platters heaped with attitudes
By loving thoughts kept warm;

A laughter laden leg of lamb
With curried fascination;
Tender talents glaze a ham,
Seasoned with elation;

Frappes of fleet flirtations;
Emotions coddled in a stew;
Feelings, thrills and mild sensations
Smoothly blended in a brew;

Profoundly pensive petits fours;
Blintzes bursting with respect;
Raptures daring youth explores
Served with honeyed intellect;

A pheasant, stuffed with childish whims,
Sedately under glass resides,
While a servant with commitment trims
A cake of bona fides;

Wonders breaded, seared and fried;
A hash of high hilarity;
A bristling broth of selfless pride;
A mousse of magnanimity;

Gravy smothered ecstasies;
Imagination pies;
Soufflés of fickle fantasies;
A chutney of surprise;

Gumbos crowned with accolades;
Mounds of meditation;
Delights that swirl in marinades
With minced deliberation;

A bisque of blatant blandishments;
Beauty blanched and then sautéed;
Charisma flavored condiments;
Memories spread with marmalade;

Frittatas of frivolity;
A roux of wild excursions;
Dumplings dunked in sophistry,
Dotted with diversions;

Chowders chocked with clever clues;
A philosophical fillet;
And pans of panoramic views
Enhance the succulent array.

A compote cooked with calm content;
And lush elusions steeped in wine.
To all are invitations sent,
Yet many foolishly decline.

Sustaining faith in frosting whipped
Coats crumpets, crisp and neat;
And piety in syrup dipped
Makes the rife repast complete.

Our gracious host, engaged in carving,
Replenishes each empty plate,
While people everywhere are starving.
Will discovery come too late?

Life's indeed a grand buffet,
As Auntie Mame would often shout.
So, join the feast and don't delay,
Lest ye be left without.

Dullness and depression wane,
When mystery and adventure call.
The curious from gloom refrain
And gather to the table all.

Sweet anticipation
Mingled with mystique
Provides us motivation
To strive for what we seek.

We nourish the body that we may survive,
But only when spirit is fed do we thrive.

AUTHOR'S COMMENT: I entered a poetry contest in which the theme was "the food of life." At first I was at a loss for inspiration. But, having played a supporting role in the musical, "Mame," I immediately focused on Auntie Mame's flamboyant exclamation that "Life is a grand buffet and yet so many poor bastards are starving." That crude remark was my inspiration for this piece.

Ugly Lamp Committee, Goshen Fair, 2000, Photo by E. G. Pizzella

ODE TO AN UGLY LAMP

Oh thou presumptuous solar pretender,
Whom I encountered while out on a bender,
What I sought was a vamp,
But I brought home a lamp
And I know not even thy gender.

Oh thou object of deepest affection,
I recall our initial connection.
Electricity flew,
But nobody knew
How I turned thee on with perfection.

Oh most unique of things that are glowing,
No emotions art thou ever showing.
You sit there so stern,
As thy filaments burn,
Divulging much less than you're knowing.

Oh thou brilliant bestower of beams,
I know nothing is quite as it seems,
But with thou I've no bitch,
On and off goes thy switch.
You're devoid of devious schemes.

Oh thou light of my life, I adore thee!
Thou dispelleth the shadows before me.
Thou giveth great pleasure,
When I readeth at leisure.
Cease never to shine, I implore thee.

Oh lantern so bright, you amaze me.
I shall always cherish and praise thee.
Though thy gargoyles of brass
May to some appear crass,
I shall ne'er let thy gaudiness phase me.

Oh thou profuse producer of glitter,
Who from viewers induces a twitter,
Though to me you have worth,
To all others on earth
Your value equates more to litter.

Oh thou disperser of nocturnal gloom,
With a flip of your switch you're in bloom.
But what gives me a fright,
When you cast forth your light,
Is you're lit, as well as the room.

Oh thou beacon so staunch and so true,
Could it be that a bird o'er thee flew,
Depositing dung,
Where crystals once hung?
Is that why your friends are so few?

Oh thou emitter of luminous glows,
You're the envy of all of my foes.
It's not that you're great,
But because of your weight
And the hope you might drop on my toes.

Oh pervasive purveyor of shine,
The sight of you weakens my spine.
Though turned off, it seems
You still light up my dreams,
Whene'er I attempt to recline.

Oh thou feckless, flamboyant flambeau,
I'm amazed at how brightly you glow.
Have you been nipping Jim Beam,
Or perhaps Irish Cream?
I'll bet you got sloshed on Cointreau!

Oh thou splendiferous spreader of luster,
It takes all of the vim I can muster
To withstand all the cracks
And the verbal attacks,
Which your critics heap on with such bluster.

Oh thou glaring stanchion of light,
I'm urged to hide thee from sight
By siblings and friends,
Who know stylish trends
And proclaim that thy presence's a blight.

Oh thou torch of such tasteless design,
In a corner I will thee confine,
For my guests you offend,
With décor you don't blend
And to regard thee I fear whilst I dine.

Oh thou source of the twilight's chagrin,
You've more wrinkles than Anthony Quinn.
I'd abandon all thrift
And get a face lift,
But, alas, you've an absence of skin.

Oh thou assault to distinguishing eyes,
You were bought as the family's surprise,
But you failed as a gift
And caused a great rift.
Now I've thee and no family ties.

Oh thou replacement for candle and flame,
Thou shalt someday garner acclaim,
Not as an antique,
Or some kind of freak,
But because this verse bears thy name.

Oh thou font of most radiant rays,
Upon treasures a robber did gaze.
To prevent larceny,
I promised him thee,
Which proves that crime never pays.

AUTHOR'S COMMENT: In the year 2000, the Goshen Fair announced that it was sponsoring an ugly lamp contest. My entry won and is displayed in the background of the above photo. I also provided the committee with a picture of my entry and this poem, which is also shown in that photo. Although I had won the contest, they nevertheless insisted on returning the lamp to me.

Photo by E. G. Pizzella

ROCK HARBOR SUNSET

Behold the beauty of a sunset, colors only God could blend,
At Rock Harbor on the Cape on a balmy autumn eve.
See the glow and feel the warmth and with solace comprehend
That which only the Creator with perfection could achieve.

Silhouettes and reflections dance and glisten in the bay,
As soft pastels on the horizon in vivid layers are neatly stacked;
Blues and pinks and purple hues heaped in colorful array,
All combine symphonicly to prove that God's a fact.

Mesmerized, we mortals are drawn to the display,
As we focus on Apollo's spectacular descent.
How appropriate a ritual to end a glorious day
And how fully has it made us feel content.

The most convincing proof of our loving God's affection
Is the sunset he provides for our visual inspection.

AUTHOR'S COMMENT: In September of 2002, we spent a weekend at Cape Cod, where we were fortunate to witness some beautiful sunsets both at Rock Harbor in Orleans and at Herring Cove near Provincetown. This is a perfect example of a concept I've developed in blending poetry with photography. It started with "The Cat At Mystic Cove" and has now moved into a scenic phase with "Rock Harbor Sunset." For this concept I coined the title "Phoetry." And this makes sense because words are merely symbols for pictures.

A PORTRAIT OF LOVE

(A poetic rendition of St. Paul's Epistle to the Corinthians)

If, with tongues of men and angels, I should glibly speak,
Withholding from my neighbor the help that he may seek,
Then I am like a boisterous bell,
Emitting sound with naught to tell,
My future as a child of God truly rendered bleak.

If I, through faith alone, a mountain could displace,
Yet of love within my heart possess not any trace,
Then I am naught but empty skin,
Devoid of substance deep within,
And banished for eternity from God's redeeming grace.

If I give all to feed the poor, appearing quite concerned,
And deliver up my body as an offering to be burned,
Yet in love be found deficient,
Wherein all should be proficient,
Not a farthing from these gestures have I earned.

Free of envy, unprovoked, love's profoundly kind,
Patient, unpretentious, putting self behind;
Is not puffed up, but unambitious,
Endowed with virtues repetitious.
It's no wonder this emotion is described as being blind.

It should come as no surprise that, always thinking good,
Love is oft by wickedness perversely understood.
Revering truth, love bears all things,
Believes and hopes and praises sings;
In purity rejoices, promoting brotherhood.

Though prophets may through age grow frail,
With tongues that cease to wag and wail,
And knowledge be destroyed,
By this be not annoyed,
So potent is the bond of love, its strength will never fail.

Sacred mysteries are unknown 'til this existence we depart.
Wise predictions seem complete, but are prophecies in part.
For what is perfect we must strive,
Though not attained while we're alive;
To face our imperfections is where love would have us start.

Children speak with childish words and childish thoughts express.
When grown, discarding childish ways, our errors we confess.
Sight, blurred by youth, then wholly clears,
Crystallized by passing years,
And our purpose of existence love demands that we address.

There's no question other traits merit our attention.
Faith and hope, for example, are worthy of our mention.
Their blessings we extol,
For they likewise lift the soul,
Endowing human character with substance and dimension.

By faith are we bestowed with endurance to abate
The onerous occurrences dealt by fickle fate.
From heaven it's been sent
To help us to repent,
That for the serpent of adversity we may not become the bait.

Hope elevates the spirit and strengthens our conviction
That goodness will prevail, dissolving hate and friction.
It supports us in our role,
To comfort and console
Those helplessly oppressed by sorrow and affliction.

Three abiding virtues thus stand out above the rest,
With which the Saints in heaven are abundantly possessed.
Faith, hope and love are they by name,
Whose merits earth and sky proclaim
And though all to heights excel, by far is love the best.

AUTHOR'S COMMENT: I have always marveled at the eloquent and inspiring language of St. Paul's epistle. It was a delight to convert it to poetic form.

TEMPUS FUGIT
[Portions based on Mt. 7.7-12]

Yield not to the pressures imposed by the crowd,
But speak your mind freely and speak it out loud.
Never give up on the power of reason
And let your hunt for integrity be ever in season.

Your talents with passion forever pursue,
But let moderation temper your view.
For your neighbor God wills you show that you care
And all of His bounty demands that you share.

To others it's written that you ought to do
What you would have them do unto you.
Give thanks for the blessings that to you are bestowed,
But be not deluded that such gifts are owed.

Pay honor to those to whom honor is due,
But forget not that you must love yourself too.
Bear not a grudge against friends or kin,
For does God not insist that we forgive those who sin.

Work hard, be resourceful and find your own way
And know in the end that dedication will pay.
Fill every moment up to the brim
And let not the light of truth ever dim.

For wound up but once is each precious life's clock
And nobody knows when the ticking will stop.

AUTHOR'S COMMENT: This poem is dedicated to my beloved sister, Louise, whose heart is enormous – and anyone who's met her knows how true that is. When I attended mass one Sunday morning, the celebrant in his sermon drew an analogy between the span of life and the operation of a spring-wound clock, saying that we must live life to its fullest because no one knows when the clock will stop ticking. I was impressed with the analogy and, when I got home, started the process of writing this poem. I finished it on my sister's birthday.

SEXUAL SEMANTICS

Why do pushy feminists torture our fair tongue·
With verbal connotations that confuse?
By their discarded bra-straps I propose that they be hung
For placing such reliance on superficial views.

Simple terminology does not affect one's rights.
Why then so much passion to offend?
Change must be accomplished in nibbles, not in bites,
If ancient institutions we are to amend.

The fact that a woman's in a leadership position
Has very little bearing on the title that's applied.
Addressing her as chairman's not a sexual description,
But merely cites the office in which she should take pride.

Making so much fuss about things of little note
Only serves to turn away those with open minds.
To constructive new approaches let us give our vote,
Using thought and intellect, instead of our behinds.

Are they simply atheists, these women of today?
Or do they trust in some eternal plan?
They emerged from Adam's rib, the scriptures clearly say,
And the name by which they're known contains a "man."

It's the basic problem that merits our attention.
Equal opportunity deserves our full support.
Why is the trivia that invariably they mention,
When there is so much substance to exhort?

Though they may argue loud and long,
Semantics won't correct what's wrong.

NOCTURNAL TREASURES

As I gazed into the heavens one crispy winter night,
Dazzled by the twinkling of the cosmic array,
I felt grateful to my Maker for the precious gift of sight,
But wondered where He hid the stars by day.

Like feelings were evoked at twilight in the fall,
When in the west a sunset stole the show.
Vivid molten hues bathed a sinking solar ball
And I queried moments later, "Where'd it go?"

Evening in the springtime is when fireflies debut,
Proclaiming their affection with random bursts of light.
Would that humans to each other might so clearly give a cue,
As do these restless bits of life in their wild nocturnal flight.

Where are these treasures hidden, while sunlit are the skies?
Cleverly concealed are they within my lady's eyes.

VIVE LA DIFFERENCE

Why does love so subjugate
And so completely rule our lives,
Causing each to seek a mate
And binding husbands to their wives?

Man, it seems, is incomplete
And of his substance needs to share.
Mistakes committed he'll repeat,
Until he finds his lady fair.

But women are a different breed,
The games they play defying reason.
Who can fathom what they need,
Or when sweet love's for them in season?

That men and women are diverse
We from birth can quickly sense,
Which spawns the essence of this verse:
Long live that difference!

THE PAUSE THAT REFRESHES

A hectic day is finally concluded
And the next impending pitfall I await.
I reflect upon the chasms I've eluded
And in a silent moment meditate.

Priorities are ordered and reviewed,
As I consider all the chores I must address.
Then my energy is mystically renewed,
For such an interlude provides relief from stress.

On one occasion when I so behaved
My VCR impelled me to applause.
I'd hit upon a way Man could be saved;
Install a button to initiate a pause!

THE PURSUIT OF HAPPINESS

One of Man's most basic rights,
It's historically been told,
Is with hope to set his sights
Upon that fabled pot of gold
And happiness in life pursue
With constant vim and zeal.
The treasure sought comes to but few,
Creating doubt it's real.

I'm convinced the more I live
That I too must have this right,
But only endless chase to give,
Left stranded in its flight,
For earthly joy and happiness
Are not for mortals to possess.

A TIMELY THEME

Of all the splendors of our earth,
Boundless riches, wealth untold,
Which possesses such great worth
That it cannot be bought or sold?

What, so precious, yet so wasted,
Is sought by those both young and old?
What, so lightly quaffed and tasted,
Is coveted by meek and bold?

Containing neither mass, nor matter,
It cannot be made or grown.
It cannot break, nor can it shatter,
Nor has it seeds that can be sown.

Borrowed sometimes, never lent,
It's paced with measured grains of sand.
Not to purchase is it spent,
But flies and never touches land.

Ever flowing, void of shape,
It lacks beginning and an end,
Yet continues to escape
The grasp of lover and of friend.

The answer to this tricky rhyme
Requires only thought and time.

AMOR EST
[Translation: Love Is]

Love is feelings gone berserk,
Emotions strained by overwork.
It's longing, wanting, needing,
Which, from the heart proceeding,
Like an avalanche of wrath,
Envelopes all within its path;
Like a tidal wave in motion,
Overwhelms with sheer devotion;
Like a volcano's fiery plumes,
Levels all, as it consumes;
And, as the phoenix from its ashes triumphantly emerges,
Deliriously bright,
A blur to human sight,
Stimulates within the breast the most delightful urges.

Love is fantasies and dreams;
Flashing lights and piercing beams;
Wild eruptions of the soul;
Total loss of self control;
Music drenched in colors bright;
Rays that puncture dark of night;
The apex of a pyramid in celestial assault;
The splendor of a rainbow, bridging heaven's vault;
The zenith of emotions in infinite progression,
Defying all attempts at definitive expression;
A gossamer illusion I ardently pursue,
Which ignites a rampant fire
Of insatiable desire,
Inviting famished eyes to feast on you.

OWED TO A PERSISTENT CREDITOR

O thou tormenter of the underdog!
O thou squeezer of the poor!
O thou clutching, grasping vulture
With thy foot stuck in the door!
Like a dog who's got a bone,
You get debtors to atone,
For tenacity is rooted in your core.

You think of them as nothing more than dirt
And this is why your attitude is curt.
Though it's a very bitter pill,
Human beings are they still,
Who have feelings that relentless chidings hurt.

It's apparent that deadbeats you abhor
And for effective types of torture you explore.
Take pity on that loathsome slug,
For deep indeed is the hole he's dug,
Yet he persists in sly diversions you deplore.

You telephone the laggard every day,
As if there were something else to say.
"Come across with the scratch,
Or your house I'll attach!"
You use every sleazy method to intimidate your prey.

You send letters 'til the mailman's feet are sore,
Which the shirker is accustomed to ignore.
Though you threaten, warn and reprimand,
He'll not respond or understand.
The job of chasing losers is an unrewarding chore.

"I hear you've been laid off, for which I sorrow.
To pay your debt it seems you'll have to borrow.
Your credit's bad?
That's really sad,
But if banks say no today, try your relatives tomorrow."

"I know that you can't pay, but what the heck;
I'll get off your case, if you'll just postdate a check."
With cynical pride
This tactic's oft tried,
Confusing the debtor and making him a wreck.

One must somehow find a method to survive.
Simply to exist demands that one contrive.
Some live from hand to mouth,
While others venture south
In search of opportunities to keep themselves alive.

Those who stay behind and fail to pack
Have learned how to withstand your vile attack.
Never does it fail.
The check is in the mail,
But the deadbeat didn't sign it, so you have to send it back.

When will the books be balanced? When will the debt be paid,
So you can drop this pretense, this act, this thin charade?
No longer will you lend,
Or credit thus extend,
But seek to earn your living in a less "demanding" trade.

To some sadistic creditors this process may be fun,
As despondent obligors the gauntlet's perils run.
Elated will they be,
Creating misery,
For what they do they do with glee, 'til gleefully it's "dun."

A POET'S WILL

While there are many who succumb
With treasures left behind,
Some pass away without a crumb,
Or with baubles none can find.

There are those who leave this earthly life
Destitute and in despair
With no product of their worldly strife
To prove that they were there.

Some have themselves interred in vaults
Of marble and of stone,
As proof that for their human faults
They did in life atone.

Some simply conjure fantasies
Of victory and of fame
To mask the empty legacies
That eulogize their name.

And last are those, the dear departed,
Who, lacking goods and heavy hearted,
Fearing dark perdition
And embarrassed by condition,
Yet seek their recognition
By trampling on tradition,
Bequeathing to posterity the singing of the birds.
But my bequest will be the best, a legacy of words.

SIMPLICITY

Simple things in a simple way
By love are magnified,
As simple words much love convey,
Which come from deep inside.

Simple words in simple ways
Do simple thoughts express
And simple thoughts, expressing praise,
Give rise to happiness.

The essentials that frequently we lack
Are simply a pat upon the back,
Or just a simple phrase
To banish one's malaise;
"You're tops in a multitude of ways.

SUPPING SEAGULLS

On a Sunday afternoon I traveled to the shore
In search of adventure and places to explore.
Stopping for a snack at the well known Dock And Dine,
My attention was attracted by what was written on a sign.

It cautioned all the patrons in letters large and red:
"Please don't feed the seagulls," it ominously said.
This was followed by a reason, which I perceived as keen:
"For if you do, they will become oppressive, wild and mean."

For a moment I was stunned and completely mystified
By that frightful admonition that I inadvertently had spied.
Thoughts of Jonathon Livingston were instantly erased
And by frenzied, savage harpies were painfully replaced.

A host of horrid images had been suggested by those words,
As suddenly I thought of Alfred Hitchcock's film, "The Birds."
Horrible attacks by winged hoards in flight
Filled the many nightmares, which tormented me that night.

I dreamt of brave Prometheus, who, against Olympic odds,
Bestowed on Man the gift of fire stolen from the gods.
Bound in chains and punished was this philanthropic giver,
As vultures circled and assailed him, feasting on his liver.

If to such a place of hazard I should e'er return,
It would only be because of my sensitive concern
For those famished, flitting creatures of the brine
And in defiance of the warning that appeared upon that sign.

THE ULTIMATE WAGER

Proof of God's existence has always been obscure,
Yet to treat the question lightly is absurd.
No one knows the answer. Of this the world was sure,
Until a savvy Frenchman spoke the final word.

Grappling with the question of whether there's a God,
The philosopher, Pascal, was flustered and distraught.
The issue was an old one, not something new and odd,
And the answer was in nothing he'd been taught.

After hours of reflection and perhaps a little sweat,
He developed a solution, which any gambler would entice.
The theory he propounded was in the nature of a bet,
The intellectual equivalent of simply casting dice.

The challenge he issued would any probing mind assuage
And the logic of his reasoning cannot be denied.
If one believes in God, proposed the artful sage,
And He indeed exists, then his salvation, of course, will be implied.

If there is credence in the Lord, on the other hand,
And our omnipotent Creator in fact does not exist,
The worst that can be said is that perhaps life may be bland
And some self-indulgent pleasures may be missed.

But if existence of our Maker one wrongfully denies
And he ignores the rules the living God's ordained,
Then the denier is condemned to perdition when he dies
And his soul will for eternity be pained.

By this simple, clever wager was the riddle thus resolved,
Exposing vital stakes in the game of life involved.

THE SECRET OF LIFE

The secret of life is in wanting to live it,
Just as with love, to receive one must give it.
But many refuse to unlock their senses
To radiant glitters that lurk behind fences.

Beauty exists in all beings on earth
And it takes but perception to see each one's worth.
Perhaps we need glasses, or our vision corrected,
To seek out the value of things unperfected.

AUTHOR'S COMMENT: I wrote this for and dedicated it to my mother on her sixty-sixth birthday. She was my beloved mentor.

REQUIEM FOR A POET

He existed for the word
And, lacking words, he soon expired.
The maze of life became absurd,
Hence his poetic soul retired.

Of veiled exotic things
He'd thought and written much.
Lowly beggars and mighty kings
Felt the impact of his touch.

Years had claimed their weary toll,
Draining strength and wit to write.
The fickle Muse had fled his soul
And with her stolen will to fight.

The wisdom of a thousand sages,
His to summon at his pleasure,
Now survives upon the pages,
Where he bequeathed to us a treasure.

Departed he this world content,
Immortalized by fate it seems,
Not in granite or cement,
But in words that conjure dreams.

A monument of eloquence
Now beams eternal rays,
Pointing out to penitents
The mystery of God's ways.

AUTHOR'S COMMENT: This poem is dedicated to the fond memory of my deceased wife's father, Phil Bittel, Sr., who, a resident of Avon, Connecticut, and because of his beautiful poetry, became known as the Bard of Avon.

THE SOUND OF THE WRITTEN WORD

The sound of the written word
Guides me in composition.
Although this may seem quite absurd,
What I write will defend my position.

The sound of the written word
Incites my innermost ear.
As I write, each syllable's heard
In tones both melodic and clear.

The sound of the written word
Sets the pattern of all that I write.
Precise become thoughts that were blurred,
Expanding my limits of sight.

The sound of the written word
Flies forth from the written page
On wings like those of a bird,
Released at last from its cage.

The sounds roll around in my head,
As I gather the thoughts I'll impart,
And thence on the page will be spread
My concept of verbal art.

What's written will no doubt astound,
When words are arranged by their sound.

CELEBRITY

By media hype created,
They're worshipped and adored.
Their virtues overrated,
Their faults are oft ignored.

By media hype created,
On pedestals they reign,
By different standards rated,
Which no one can explain.

By media hype created,
Their life's an open book
And frequently they're baited
To bite firmly on the hook.

By media hype created,
With no secrets to possess,
Their privacy's debated
By members of the press.

By media hype created,
Yet fate is often cruel
And, though well compensated,
They sometimes play the fool.

By media hype created,
They're subject to attacks
By fans they've motivated,
Who lack essential facts.

By media hype created,
Part human, part divine,
First loved, then fiercely hated,
They walk a narrow line.

PICKING OUT A BEAU

Drole indeed is the female mind,
When it comes to her choice of a mate.
Acting as though she's emotionally blind,
She'll leave issues of substance to fate.

She'll always come up with a loser,
No matter how many she meets;
A gambler, a beater, a boozer,
Or a guy whose home is the streets.

Never a man of distinction,
A man who merits respect.
She's neither concerned with his diction,
Nor the depth of his intellect.

If he's committed a multiple murder,
Or is in jail on a felony count,
She'll tingle with frivolous fervor
And the rate of her heart beat will mount.

But if he's only a hard working sap,
Who'll treat her with gentle concern,
Who'd never give her a slap,
Then this is the sort she will spurn.

If there's one thing most women don't know,
It's the right way to pick out a beau.

SEA SENSE

When I find myself beleaguered and my spirits hit a low,
I pause and head directly to the beach.
There I meditate in leisure and revive my inner glow
And annoyances remove beyond my reach.

Looking seaward, I'm enveloped by the vast expanse of blue,
As rolling breakers in sequence reveal their pearly caps.
While the horizon strives to separate shades of azure hue,
Waves relentlessly chastise the shore with repetitious slaps.

At the edge of the Atlantic I'm pacific and I'm free
And clarity of thought is quickly found,
For I listen to those ripples and hear the restless sea
And at that very moment see the sound.

'Tis on the sandy shore that tranquility I find,
Clearing all the cobwebs from my mind.

BEAUTY'S WHY AND WHEREFORE

What, pray tell, is Beauty's chief design?
'Tis a question that I've pondered deep and long.
Does it trace its source to origins divine,
Or does its existence to pure happen-stance belong?

Is Beauty's purpose to give joy to those who view,
Or to fill the heart of its creator with delight?
Does it belong to the many or the few?
Or does it merely seek envy to incite?

Does it lie dormant in the eye of the beholder,
Or with flames of inspiration does it glow?
Does it exhort its admirers to grow bolder,
Since Shelley said it's "all ye need to know?"

Alas, with Emerson I find myself agreeing
That "Beauty is its own excuse for being."

AUTHOR'S COMMENT: I wanted to write something inspiring to commemorate my grandson, Aaron's high school graduation. When I came across Emerson's poem, "The Rhodora," I was so enraptured by its eloquence that I grabbed a pen and VOILA!

A VISIT WITH FRIENDS

We packed up our stuff and cleaned up the car
And prepared for our trip to east Maine.
Although our destination was far,
We vowed that we'd not complain.

When Charles we met at his country abode,
We realized we needed a scale.
His baggage comprised most of our load,
With nine melons he purchased on sale.

We made up our minds, Charles, Shirley and Ed,
That we would escape summer's heat.
At Charlotte we knew we'd be welcomed and fed
By our most gracious host, Nick Battit.

Driving so far can cause quite a strain
And this made us feel insecure,
But the distance was nothing compared to the pain
Of the puns Charles made us endure.

We shared many pleasant and jovial times,
Admiring the New Brunswick shore.
In the evening we'd chat and Ed read his rhymes
And Campobello was fun to explore.

Jean proudly displayed her sculpturing skill
And with laughter she nearly exploded,
As time after time Ed rounded the hill
With driftwood heavily loaded.

Brother Charles acted worse than most felons.
His behavior was pitifully sad.
He forced us to eat all his melons
For fear that they might go bad.

Hummus was served with pine nuts and bread
And to linguisa and eggs we awoke.
Blueberry sundaes prepared us for bed,
But at the mention of melons we'd choke.

Ed posed the group for photos bizarre
And Shirley served savory steak.
It was a chore getting driftwood into the car,
But at dusk we'd cruise on the lake.

Amazed by the beauty of FDR's retreat,
We picnicked overlooking the bay.
Feasting on sandwiches made with crabmeat,
We watched loons in the sunset at play.

At Reversible Falls, while homeward bound,
A yard sale came into sight.
You'll never guess what Shirley found,
Plastic tulips that actually light.

Meeting the Fosters we all felt was keen.
They seemed like a gaggle of fun.
Their cottage was out of a magazine.
When they met, Joanie pinched Warren's "bum."

A visit with friends
In truth never ends.
But, as snows follow fall,
Provides dreams to recall
And, without lavish frills,
It leaves memories to warm winter's chills.

AUTHOR'S COMMENT: Our friends, Nick and Jean Battit lived in East Hampton, but had a quaint summer retreat on a lake called Round Pond in northern Maine. One summer they invited us to spend a few days with them there and we enjoyed our visit immensely. After that, we visited them there several more times and the next piece is a sequel.

ROUND POND REVISITED

It's said that a sequel can never compare
To the thrill of the first enterprise,
But our subsequent visit to Jean and Nick's lair
Clearly proves that such statements are lies.

On our way I shouted, "Get me a shrink,"
As I pointed ahead in surprise.
On a flatbed a gingerbread house painted pink
Overwhelmed our incredulous eyes.

Before this odd sight got too far ahead,
My camera I placed in Shu's hand.
"Shoot through the windshield," I hurriedly said
And she quickly obeyed my command.

With this ominous sign we consulted our maps
And proceeded eastward in Maine.
We knew that regardless of any mishaps
Our journey would not be in vain.

At a tollbooth I stopped and found it was closed.
No attendant there could I find.
My companion chided that I must have dozed,
While a line was forming behind.

Our day of departure had started out bright
And continued as northward we strove.
At noon there was fog, which hampered our sight,
As east on the airline we drove.

When Calais we reached and asked for direction,
A chill had replaced the sun's balmy glows.
Seeking my jacket, I made an inspection
And found I'd forgotten my clothes.

A store that sells clothing is what we then sought,
But only a food store came into sight.
There a gray sweatshirt I happily bought,
Which served as my wardrobe each morning and night.

When we went up to the clerk to pay for my prize,
We recounted our woes with dismay.
The laughter evoked brought tears to her eyes
And she blurted that we'd made her day.

As we passed o'er a bridge that was under repair,
Shirley urged me to step on the brake.
She took pictures of ducks that were swimming there,
As the fog rolled in on the lake.

We finally arrived at renowned Camp Battit
And, as expected, our quarters were nice.
We relaxed and, when it came time to eat,
Jean cooked up some great Spanish rice.

After enjoying this flavorful dish,
Jean showed us a sculpture that looked like a horse.
Since it also possessed a tail like a fish,
We dubbed it Seabiscuit, of course.

To Cobscook Bay Park we four took a ride,
Attended a lecture, then toured every part.
"The eagle's been saved," said the ranger with pride
And he brought out an eagle named Bart.

Bart was a large and impressive old bird.
In his youth he'd been wounded and lost his left wing.
To give him his freedom was clearly absurd,
So at lectures like this he's the king.

A table we found with a view of the cove
And snacked on ham sandwiches made with dark bread.
Then back to the camp we leisurely drove,
Looking forward to what lay ahead.

A large hunk of driftwood Jean pulled from her batch,
Which resembled an eagle high on its perch.
Its missing left wing she hoped to attach,
If she should prevail in her search.

Without this prosthesis, which she would append
To this very unique piece of art,
It looked very much like our fine feathered friend,
The eagle the ranger called Bart.

Unlike that poor bird, mental images soared
And elation appeared in our tone:
"Let this coincidence not be ignored.
Call it Bart and leave it alone!"

Later the group was invited to dine
At the Fosters' lovely abode.
Joannie's sumptuous vittles were simply divine
And we ate 'til we thought we'd explode.

Welcomed with buckets of booze and a squeeze,
We viewed all the work brother Arthur had done.
Our cordial reception had put us at ease,
So we chatted and joked and had oodles of fun.

Joannie's hors d'oeuvres would tempt any palate.
Her crab cakes and ribs were a treat.
A hot lobster bisque and then a fruit salad
Made our evening repast complete.

Up to this juncture our trip had been great
And we knew why we'd traveled so far.
When the party broke up, it was getting late
And it poured as we ran to the car.

The following dawn brought cause for alarm.
Shirley's Elf had dropped in the rain.
We were relieved, when we found that no harm
Had come to her camera and photos of Maine.

On the City of Eastport we focused our sights
And there eagerly went to survey.
We were awed by its charm, its visual delights
And vivid hues in abundant array.

Liberally dabbed with colorful paint,
As if to dissipate drabness and fears,
Its buildings were charming, historic and quaint,
Snugly wrapped in its harbor and piers.

The Pleon appeared self-centered and smug,
As it sat with a grin in its slip.
Its colors foretold this diminutive tug
Could tow the most grandiose ship.

The six of us met for lobsters and such
In a restaurant with fresh pine décor.
We were all enjoying our meal very much,
'Til stunned by a shattering roar.

We looked out of the window in shock
And from our seats were nearly expelled.
A huge metal ferry hung up on a rock
Was the image our eyes then beheld.

They've come up with a new way of docking here.
They just run the vessel aground.
It saves the substantial cost of a pier,
But sure makes a God awful sound.

We said our goodbyes. It was now time to leave.
Our fond recollections would fill up a tome.
We accomplished all we set out to achieve
And the time had come to go home.

Heading south on Route 1, we departed,
Bound for a place where Shirley once dined.
Town after town we drove through heavy hearted,
For this restaurant we nowhere could find.

My companion was stubborn and I was appalled,
For we now had entered a neighboring state.
'Twas Yoken's at Portsmouth, the Mecca recalled,
Its discovery due solely to fate.

A visit with friends,
In truth, never ends,
But leaves glowing an ember
We'll always remember,
No matter which way the path bends.

TEMPTATION'S CALL

Being poor, I've learned to live with less
And I'm thankful for the little that I've got.
But there are times, when, frankly I confess,
I'm envious of those who have a lot.

When invited out to dine, I was taught
To make my portion small and seek no more.
Bargains are responsible for most of what I've bought
And I've learned to shop around from store to store.

I'm modest in the style in which I live.
My house is small, my car is old and I must toil each day.
Of necessity I limit what in charity I give
And I'm used to taking home a meager pay.

In most of life's vain luxuries I've practiced self-denial,
Which has strengthened me for problems I must face.
When I analyze my life and place myself on trial,
There's little that in hindsight I'd erase.

But when it comes to being kissed,
The bastions of frugality in total ruin fall,
For the only thing, in truth, I absolutely can't resist
Is amorous temptation's siren call.

SURRENDER?

We saw terror in the sky,
As those lofty towers crumbled,
But such attacks we must defy
And let our spirits not be humbled.

Yes, we took a nasty blow,
But our way of life survives.
We must stand up to the foe
And resume our normal lives.

Patriotic feeling's high
And we see flags where're we go,
Yet we're still afraid to fly.
Are those colors merely show?

If we allow ourselves to stiffen up with fright,
The flags we wave might just as well be white.

AUTHOR'S COMMENT: After the 9/11 attack many people were
afraid to fly, fearing that their plane might be hijacked by terrorists.
That fear was the inspiration for this sonnet.

Photo by E. G. Pizzella

PHOENIX AND THE FELINE

In the State of Arizona there's a city,
Whose name has vital ties with every kitty.
Mythology's to blame
For that famous urban name
And its origin's the subject of this ditty.

It's not geography with which we're here concerned,
But with a bird that's accustomed to be burned.
Teasing our imagination
With its feats of immolation
Is this fabled mythic foul of which we've learned.

It's the Phoenix of the sky that interests me,
Not the handle of that urban entity.
Mystically it burned,
As to ashes it was turned,
And gone forever up in smoke it seemed to be.

Then from naught it would suddenly arise
And regenerate before your very eyes,
Appearing quite unharmed
And not at all alarmed,
As upward in the blue it swiftly flies.

Let's now compare this to our furry feline friends,
For both excel in multiplicity of ends.
But hapless cat must confine
The number of its lives to nine,
Which my sense of fairness unequivocally offends.

Why on earth should this feathered myth possess
Successive avian lives in such excess,
While to our household pet we give
Only nine for him to live?
For reform of this inequity, we all should strongly press!

Consider how this impacts basic fairness in our land.
It's something all good liberals should clearly understand.
In the field of aviation
We've revealed discrimination
And to our trusting felines we must lend a helping hand.

Since the flight path of the Phoenix extends to outer space,
As to where one might complain, I'd say NASA is the place.
Discrimination's not allowed!
It's a rule of which we're proud,
And this injustice we'll endeavor to erase.

PROLOGUE TO ETERNITY
(Based on Dante's "Inferno")

"A portal am I to the Sorrowful City,
Where agony reigns and suffering's eternal.
Inviting lost souls to wallow in pity,
I furnish the ultimate passage infernal.

"To build me, my Maker, by Justice compelled,
Harnessed Love's power, supreme and divine
And, coupled with Knowledge nowhere excelled,
Completed a matchless and perfect design.

"Before my creation, nothing existed
And I am eternal and always will be.
No matter how fiercely you've fought and resisted,
Abandon all hope when you enter me."

These are the words inscribed o'er the gate
Through which those condemned are ushered by fate.

AUTHOR'S COMMENT: It's one thing to translate poetry. It's another
to cast the translation in poetic form. I find this literary exercise truly
exhilarating. Following is the inscription above the gate of Hell in
Dante's "Inferno":

"Per me si va nella citta dolente;
Per me si va nel eterno dolore;
Per me si va tra la perduta gente.
Giustizia mosse il mio alto Fattore.
Fecemi la Divina Potestate,
La Somma Sapienza e'l Primo Amore.
Dinanzi a me non fuor' cose create,
Se non io, ed io eterna duro.
Lasciate ogni speranza voi ch'entrate."

PATHOLOGY

The road to hell, by nature's law,
Is paved with good intentions.
In each of us exists this flaw,
Which bears unique dimensions.

Resulting guilt one may conceal,
Which gnaws at every heart.
While I pursued a world unreal,
My real world fell apart.

Plans that oft were well intended
Bore but meager fruit.
Great successes, all pretended,
Did naught but loneliness recruit.

Time that's lost can't be replaced,
As things that break repaired,
Nor can sadness be erased
By knowing someone cared.

The moral here's a timeless theme,
Which I'm compelled to borrow.
Mellowed by tomorrow's dream
Is pain of bygone sorrow.

If the path to Satan's door with good intent is paved,
Of what composed is that by which we're saved?

ODE TO A FOUR-LETTER WORD

O most wondrous of words! How often art thou used
In films and books, shyly whispered, frequently abused?
How pretentious must thou be,
Importing care in each degree?
It's no wonder those affected are confused.

O most powerful of lingual exclamations,
Applied to intimate and casual relations,
The likes of thou should be precise,
Or otherwise we're rolling dice.
Severely limited should be thy connotations.

O utterance of wide and varied means,
Repeated oft by ancients and by teens,
Ensembles soon commence to crumble,
When the only word mouths mumble
Fails properly to indicate, where the mumbler leans.

How can a simple word such different meanings tell,
From lust to care for animals and relatives as well?
Does verbal scarcity exist,
Or has a basic flaw been missed?
All should hasten such a mystery to dispel.

A word, which such broad tenor doth impart,
Loses force, although spoken from the heart.
I suggest new words we frame,
For surely this one's gotten lame
And persistence in its use puts the horse behind the cart.

For connubial affection "love" alone should be applied,
While "cherish" seems to work for knots more loosely tied,
As for relatives and mothers,
Friends and neighbors, pets and others,
Being all platonic, nothing more can be implied.

To enunciate concern for things immobile or inert,
Try "favor," "like," or "relish," as for instance with desert.
A lexiconic system, so cleverly devised,
Should quickly be adopted and widely publicized
To distinguish those enamored from those who merely flirt.

MARTYRS?

They boast that they are martyrs in their cause,
That their goal is to carry out God's will,
And confederates offer their applause
For the malicious objectives they fulfill.

They're revered as martyrs by their peers,
As they subvert and clandestinely conspire,
But do martyrs torture innocents with fears
And is murder of the guiltless their desire?

Twisted spawns of hatred's vile seduction,
They've commenced a diabolical crusade.
Islam seeks not slaughter and destruction.
Their religion they have blatantly betrayed.

The proof is senseless mayhem they've inflicted
And the nightmares that time will not erase.
By the wounded towers they're convicted,
For their rancid smoke depicts the devil's face.

AURHOR'S COMMENT: This poem was inspired by a spectacular photo appearing in the Hartford Courant at the time of the September 11th attack. It depicted the twin towers on fire with thick black smoke pouring out of the buildings, the smoke clearly forming an image, which unmistakably resembled what is generally perceived to be the face of Satan.

ANATOMY OF A BOYCOTT

History is the greatest teacher known,
Which history itself has clearly shown.
Ancient Rome, for example,
Where oddities were ample,
Is a garden in which legends have been sown.

When relations between the classes became tense
And it seemed that a war would soon commence,
Agrippa entered on the scene,
Boldly stepping in between,
And with this tale made his appeal to common sense.

"The human body is of many parts comprised.
What if one of them was by the rest despised?
Havoc surely would ensue
To dismay this hapless crew
And total ruination might soon be realized.

"The body's members differ in function, shape and size,
From hands to feet to shoulders, mouth and eyes.
Suppose the stomach, satisfied,
Proceeded other parts to chide,
Provoking and inciting them in anger to arise.

"'The stomach's in the middle,' the other organs thought.
'We work to feed it, while it sits there doing naught!'
Jealous envy then would swell,
Causing others to rebel,
And a strike against the stomach would thus be sought.

"All the other parts with venom would conspire
And from performing their assignments might retire.
The boycott then would be complete
From top of head down to the feet
And the situation at that point would then be dire.

"To gather food hands and fingers would decline
And cause the mouth in its functions to resign.
Where once the body flourished,
It would now be undernourished
And toward starvation it swiftly would incline.

"Without food for the stomach to digest,
There'd be no nutrients to feed the hungry rest.
The truth would then rise to the fore,
Which all had failed to see before,
And their mutual dependence would clearly be expressed."

This lesson the combatants quickly heeded.
'Twas not dissension, but unity they needed.
"We hang together and unite,
Lest separate hangings be our plight,"
Became the motto they collectively repeated.

Let the impact of wisdom never cease,
But may its influence ever more increase,
And though to some it seems absurd,
Here's proof that through a simple word
Violence and destruction may decrease

ETERNAL CITY

Alba Longa prospered under Proca's peaceful reign,
To which his elder son was by custom to succeed.
But the younger of his offspring he lacked power to restrain,
For Amulius sought by force to take the lead.

Now his brother had three children nearly grown,
Who were happy to accept their lot in life.
But their uncle was suspicious of the harm that might be sown,
If these should secretly incite rebellious strife.

The would-be usurper his two nephews ordered slain
To remove all competition from the field.
No threat to his ascension at this point did now remain,
Save the issue which his niece some day might yield.

To be certain she'd not bear a baby boy
A vestal virgin this maid he did appoint.
Then removing his brother by clever trick and ploy,
Officiously as ruler did he himself anoint.

Smooth sailing oft eludes those bent on selfish gain
And so it came to pass in this event,
For a circumstance arose, which caused the tyrant pain,
And he sought avidly to soothe his discontent.

The virgin had been ravished and spawned a set of twins,
A pair of sons, who posed a regal threat,
And this is where the story of a citadel begins,
A tantalizing tale none can forget.

The niece claimed that her sons were of origin divine.
It's not known if she believed that this was true,
But it none-the-less caused shivers up and down the despot's spine,
So he ordered her removed from public view.

By loyal friends abducted, the infant sons of Mars
Were taken to the Tiber and in darkness set afloat.
Little did they know what was written in the stars,
As they drifted on the tide in a basket for a boat.

Adopted by a she-wolf, when they landed, were the pair
And she nurtured them as though they were her own.
Grown to be young men, they exited the lair
And settled at the site that would be Rome.

The crowns of seven hills they encompassed in their view,
As with fervor they began to build a fortress tall.
But in a fit of anger Romulus his brother slew,
When Remus, in derision, with ease leapt o'er the wall.

A ring around the seven hills Romulus then drew
And the land within he walled and set apart.
Here a truly charismatic and eternal city grew,
Which of western culture came to be the heart.

Another version placed the boys in the rustic home
Of a simple rugged shepherd and his wife.
There they grew and organized an army to dethrone
The villain, who had tried to take their life.

If their nurturing requires a bit more clarity,
Their stepmother, historians disclose,
Free-spirited was thought by her peers to be,
From whence the nick-name "she-wolf" thus arose.

Restoring their mother's father to the throne,
For Amulius, the despot, had been killed,
They returned to the place where they had grown,
A new and greater city there to build.

Whatever be the source of this historic place,
Romantic or exotic or mundane,
It brings to every traveler a smile upon his face,
Who with memory of its image boards his plane.

Of a vast and far flung empire this metropolis was head
With its Ceasars in command beneath the senate's dome.
Is it any wonder that through the ages it's been said
That invariably all roads must lead to Rome?

Its alluring attributes are everywhere renowned
And its leadership in fashion's unsurpassed.
A tourist who visits is no longer homeward bound
And here a stringent diet cannot last.

So beguiling is this place that, when strangers come to stay,
It's said that they must act as Romans do.
Its architectural marvels were not constructed in a day,
But more likely took a century or two.

It's ironic that this city, which before our savior's birth
Conquered all the world by force of arms,
Now subjugates and rules all the nations of the earth
Through its culture, beauty, art and ancient charms.

ARTISTIC DIFFERENCES

How does one distinguish
Businessmen from men of art?
'Tis a question that's been posed
Both to dull of wit and smart.

A businessman's concerned with now.
Tomorrow's out of sight.
Birds in bushes he ignores,
But the one in hand holds tight.

He'll peddle any kind of ware,
If in it there's a buck.
Cutting corners to advance,
He'll not rely on luck.

He's stoic, stern and cynical,
Viewing others with a squint,
And never takes a peek at life
Through glasses of rose tint.

An artist's just the opposite.
With now he cannot cope.
He deals in terms of someday,
In the future finding hope.

From reality he steps aside,
Abhorring plots and schemes.
While others face the gruesome truth,
He hides his head in dreams.

A businessman is prone to stress,
Resulting in poor health.
An artist lives from day to day,
Unconcerned with wealth.

Although they seem quite far apart,
On one thing they agree;
Selling is a form of art
And art sells for a fee.

FRECKLES

Freckles have been the subject o'er the years
Of many jokes, which callously are made.
Some create annoyance, even tears,
And folks have felt belittled or betrayed.

Such blemishes ought not to make one sad,
For the trait is one genetically bestowed.
They're a part of one's appearance, good or bad,
And therefore no apologies are owed.

To the end that they may never cause one pain,
Or became the source of sorrow or depression,
I submit that they are easy to explain
And offer this definitive expression:

Freckles are a sign from God above,
Each a tiny imprint of His love.

CAT-ATUDE

For eons they've been toasted
As Man's most devoted friend
And their owners thus have boasted
Merits they cannot defend.

So, I ask now, "What's the difference
Between the canine and the cat?"
Well, the answer's based on inference
Drawn from attitude, not fact.

When the owner of a mutt
Pays attention to his beast,
The pooch will bark and shake his butt,
His rapture thus to be unleashed.

And when food and shelter are provided,
A dog will certainly opine:
"No doubt my welfare's been confided
To one who's obviously divine!"

While demanding no attention,
A cat, who's posed in such a stance,
Assumes a look of condescension
And this comment would advance:

"Thanks for all that you've bestowed,
But treat us felines not as odd,
For it's to us that tribute's owed –
Do you not recognize your God?"

INSPIRED BY THE MEWS

Once I met a cat at Mystic Cove
And by that critter so intrigued was I
That into my mystic world of words I quickly dove
To find descriptive terms that would apply.

With pen in hand, I profusely sought to glorify
His effervescent charm and feline verve
And with my camera lens I would deftly try
His unique image to capture and preserve.

His behavior appeared to me quite strange,
For he cooperated to the nth degree.
He placed his snout within my Kodak's range
And thus the photo I obtained was blemish free.

When I returned I captured him in rhyme,
Memorializing each distinctive trait.
The result was a composite so sublime
That its sequel I now anxiously await.

That by this creature I was mesmerized is plain
And this he seemed instinctively to know.
I'm at a loss however to explain
How he captivated and impressed me so.

To attract my attention no contrivance did he use,
I was simply inspired by the mews.

AURHOR'S COMMENT: This poem is a sequel to The Cat At Mystic Cove, which appears on page 64.

BELATED BLAME

It's said that years ago Pandora caused a massive toxic spill,
Which blemished every living thing on land, in sea and air.
Though centuries have elapsed, the results are with us still
And the planet now requires much repair.

Although this was an incident of obvious pollution,
Never from the liberals was there whimper or complaint.
This problem, none-the-less, requires a solution,
For all the world now suffers from its taint.

It poses, in addition, a case of clear discrimination,
Which in this era of equality has never been addressed.
Of this deplorable event there's been no investigation
And the need for due inquiry must be diligently pressed.

If a male had been responsible for this malicious deed,
Bold would be the headlines in accord with current trends.
Does the fact that she was female in her favor intercede?
If so, my sense of fairness such hypocrisy offends.

In their quest for equal rights, when with vim they tout their worth,
Let's with subtlety remind them that a woman spoiled the earth.

AUTHOR'S COMMENT: For a piece with a similar theme, see "The Mother Of Spills" at page 259.

DIMPLED CHAD CHICANERY

Butterfly ballots are said to be confusing
And voters have punched twice, when once will do.
To throw them out the Democrats are stubbornly refusing,
For this would mean their votes would then be few.

The Veep is always harping that every vote should count,
Even though the ballot is unclear.
Counting all the dimples will make his tallies mount,
Which is precisely what Republicans all fear.

Recounts and lawsuits cause others to make fun
Of our election process, which is sad.
But the man who will take office in the year 2001
Will be chosen by a slightly dimpled chad.

To accord the people's will its proper clout,
The ballot must be free of any doubt.

AUTHOR'S COMMENT: In the national election of 2000 between George W. Bush and Al Gore, who served as Vice President under Bill Clinton, there were disputes over how to deal with ballots containing "dimpled chads." See the related piece entitled, "Electoral Depression" at page 223.

ELECTORAL DEPRESSION

Depression is caused no doubt by stress
Among the population far and wide
And it's been heightened by an odd election mess,
Which assures that the illness won't subside.

But the depression that disturbs this feeble mind
Is a condition that really makes me mad.
It's not an ailment that afflicts our humankind,
But the depression of a slightly dimpled chad.

This tortured bit, this cousin to a dent,
Is the product of a sloppy human hand
And will likely choose our nation's President,
The leader of our vast beloved land.

Be mindful that when weighty problems mount,
It's little things apparently that count.

MY LAPTOP

I've got a laptop I adore,
Which greets me every morn.
Many worlds do we explore
And without it I'm forlorn.

I've got a laptop I adore,
Which I position on my knee.
Then my coffee I will pour,
Amused by boundless energy.

I've got a laptop I adore,
Which responds to every touch.
I never know just what's in store,
But it's now become a crutch.

I've got a laptop I adore,
Which I fondle day and night.
It will never be a bore,
'Cause our relationship is tight.

I've got a laptop I adore.
It drives me to distraction.
Yet it's a thing I can't ignore,
For it gives me satisfaction.

I've got a laptop I adore,
Which makes my life worthwhile.
My ailing id does it restore
And causes me to smile.

I've got a laptop I adore.
It demands my full attention.
Ne'er will I be like before,
Because of this invention.

I've got a laptop I adore,
Which weighs but several pounds.
Its operation's not a chore,
But it makes the oddest sounds.

I've got a laptop I adore,
Whose buttons I will often tweak.
It will always beg for more,
As it proceeds to purr and squeak.

I've got a laptop I adore,
Though out of date is its design.
Modern versions I deplore,
For I'm content with mine.

I've got a laptop I adore
And, having had our little chat,
I'll not mislead you anymore.
My laptop is my cat.

AUTHOR'S COMMENT: Simpson was an amazing cat. He died at the age of 20. Shirley taught him every trick in the book. He could "give paw" and "clean paw." He would even hold what we called "rock concerts." Shirley would sit him on the bed and in front of him place a stone and another common object, like a cup. Then she would name the two objects and tell him to place his paw on one or the other. To our astonishment he was able to distinguish between the two and would place his paw on the one she named. Every morning he would jump up on her lap and kiss her nose, so we referred to him as her laptop. We were devastated when he died.

A THOUSAND WORDS

To tell a tale the mind excites,
Like Homer, Dante and many more,
Is the goal on which I've set my sights,
A wistful realm that I'd explore.

Rockwell's one whom all admire.
He graced the covers of the Post
With expressive images that inspire,
A trait which I would love to boast.

Inciting passion in mankind
Through precious works of art
Is what our maker had in mind,
When creation He did start.

Like Hitchcock's film that's called "The Birds,"
A picture's worth a thousand words.

PROLIFIC PIXELS

What's the value of a picture?
It's been asked so many times
And tritely answered with a mixture
Of garbled prose and silly rhymes.

Well, I offer this solution,
Though it's nothing very new.
It's been known since evolution
And, what's more, I think it's true.

From an image spring impressions,
Like flocks of frenzied, fleeing birds,
Giving rise to the contention,
"A picture's worth a thousand words."

What most fail to understand,
And on those who teach I place the blame,
Is that words are merely a command
To call up visions by their name.

Alas, I've found the answer, for which my ego swells.
A picture's worth equates to the story that it tells.
So, never let us consciously underestimate
The emotional eruptions an image can create.

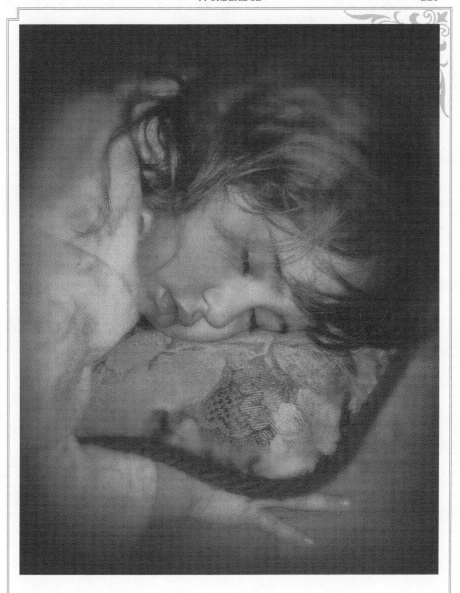

LILY'S SONG

The first day of March was chilled by a breeze
And I looked out the window at gray, barren trees,
As I longed for the green that colors fresh peas
And the floral aromas that lure flirting bees.

Confined to my office with Lawyer's disease,
Penurious clients I forced to their knees,
While from their purses trying to squeeze
What most would consider exorbitant fees.

Answering the phone, what I heard made me freeze,
For born was a Bayer named Lily Louise,
A pink and delightful feminine tease,
Designed by the Lord her parents to please.

Happy, indeed, were Libro and Weeze,
For this joyous event their fears did appease.
My poetic bent it did suddenly seize,
So I grabbed up my pen and this verse wrote with ease:

"May she happily romp through hills, vales and leas,
Ever avoiding corruption and sleaze.
When she's hit by a blow, let that blow be a sneeze
And may her intellect earn her scores of degrees.
To a chest full of gold may she acquire the keys
And may the Lord up above hear all of her pleas."

AUTHOR'S COMMENT: Louise, sometimes referred to as Weeze, is
my sister, who's married to Libro. When their daughter, Maria Bayer,
gave birth to her daughter, Lily, I wrote this poem to commemorate
her birth.

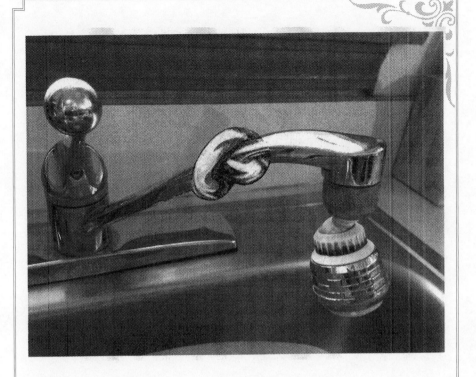

MY FAVORITE PLUMBER

I hired my son Steven to fix my faucet's leak,
Unaware that by the Muse he had been kissed.
With his trusty plumber's wrench I expected him to tweak,
Not to give it such an ostentatious twist.

When I grumbled that water from this tap would never pour,
He beamed with that snicker we all know.
"To simply stop the drip, you told me was my chore,
It's extra now to make the water flow."

A sense of humor is essential in every path that we pursue
And Steven is the proof of what I say.
That he takes pride in his work is obviously true,
But he also gets his kicks along the way.

The two most precious qualities I see within my son
Are the skill with which he toils and his jests when work is done.

AUTHOR'S COMMENT: My eldest son, Steve, is a plumbing contractor. He's a marvelous plumber with a fantastic sense of humor. I thought he would enjoy this twist.

MY SECOND BORN

The twentieth of December
Is a date that I'll remember,
For on that day,
I'm proud to say,
Was born a very special family member.

A chubby blue-eyed blond was my son, Rick,
Who, when a child, at times was sick.
Suffering from the colic,
'Twas little cause for frolic
And we wondered if the Lord had played a trick.

Such fussing and crying we had never seen
And the medicine prescribed was Kelly green.
Because of him we couldn't sleep,
So in the bathroom went the creep
And the doctor confirmed this wasn't mean.

The picture in my mind still clearly clings
Of an ever jolting sack of shifting springs.
When I fed this babe his bottle,
It was like I pulled the throttle
On a Model T equipped with flying wings.

We were frequently awakened with a fright,
Hearing scraping sounds and thuds throughout the night.
When Rick was still quite small,
He'd rock his crib from wall to wall
And then he'd greet us in the morning with delight.

I remember when the kids helped build the pool
On a summer night, when they were out of school.
Rick was walking on the rim
And with a light in hand fell in,
Giving us a fright I thought was cruel.

His love of chocolate was a matter of renown.
With a chocolate cake I've seen him go to town.
"Happy Birthday" we'd all sing,
Then he'd eat the whole damned thing.
He always found a way to be a clown.

Gizmos to this character appealed
And his knack for mechanics was revealed.
With brother Steven he'd conspire,
Rigging booby traps with wire,
When they were not out playing baseball in the field.

His aptitude for knowledge became clear
And at an early age did wit appear.
He knew well how to have fun.
He could quickly turn a pun
And was in the realm of humor without peer.

He learned his lessons well, I must confess,
With college grades that surely would impress.
This boy, who was so dear,
Became an engineer,
Relieving me at last of all my stress.

AARON'S SONG

We see good folks and we see fakes,
Who repeat their old mistakes,
And we learn by the process of comparin'.

Problems bother us each day.
Some are solved and others stay,
And at our gut a vital question's always tearin'.

What's a family all about?
I can say without a doubt
That its essence is selflessness and sharin'.

Without strainin' very hard
I could cite, in this regard,
Its synonym, which, of course is carin'.

Now, when siblings help eachother,
As with a sister or a brother,
This lightens up the burden both are bearin'.

And when one protects the other,
As would a father or a mother,
That takes a lot of fortitude and darin'.

A family certainly has clout,
If they don't sit around and pout,
And no effort for the group should they be sparin'.

When they embark upon a trip,
They're like shipmates on a ship
And to attain their mutual goals are always rarin',

Thus has a boy grown from a child
And, though he bears the name of "Wild,"
By his name be not beguiled,
For, with a temperament that's mild,
He mirrors these ideals. Thank God for Aaron!

AUTHOR'S COMMENT: I wrote this for my grandson, Aaron Wild, when he was a youngster. Having graduated from Yale University and Johns Hopkins Medical School, he is now in residency at Sloan Kettering in New York.

EXPRESSIONS OF LOVE

We manifest emotions in a multitude of ways;
Happiness by giggles, laughs and smiles;
Sadness, or what some may call malaise,
By tears and fearful frowns observed for miles.

Of all our human feelings love vaults to the fore,
As that, which in its methods of expression,
Permits each individual freely to explore
With every novel nuance and dimension.

Love can be conveyed by just a look,
A touch, a word, a plethora of deeds.
Proclamations of love can fill a book,
For clearly love fulfills so many needs.

That declarations of love are truly ample
This verse aptly serves as an example.

THE FICTION OF ADDICTION

Self restraint in any form is something liberals fear,
Though it's the virtue of our forbears that got us where we are.
Discipline's essential in building a career
And without it one will not go very far.

Lack of self control is now termed an addiction
To dodge the blame for evil things we do.
Those leaning toward the left rely upon this fiction
That licentiousness we may with impunity pursue.

If harm should flow from drinking to excess,
Or from gambling or sexual deviation,
The foible we may guiltlessly confess,
Since the condition must require medication.

Temptation we need not in this modern day defy!
Why deprive ourselves of momentary pleasure?
It may on some occasions be more practical to lie,
Rather than to forfeit any treasure.

Weakness of the will is no longer recognized
As a flaw for which one may justly be chastised.

LOVE OF A RAINY DAY

I just love a rainy day.
I lounge in bed and debate if I should rise,
As loving sheets embrace my lazy thighs,
But reason comes at last and leads the way.

I just love a rainy day.
I bear the look of one insane,
As I gaze transfixed through every pane,
Viewing dripping, wrinkled objects in array.

I just love a rainy day.
As windswept flurries wave and pass,
Distorting images on the glass,
Which seem determined to join the muddled fray.

I just love a rainy day,
Especially when it's in the spring
And droplets cover everything
In preparation for nature's verdant art display.

I just love a rainy day,
When vain diversions are subdued
That chores neglected may be cued
By lightening, thunder, overcast and gray.

I just love a rainy day,
When no longer can I stall,
For I'm compelled to heed the call
Of obligations to which attention I must pay.

I just love a rainy day,
For at last I feel relieved
By accomplishments achieved,
And, guiltless, I can now resume my play.

Rain benefits not only things that grow,
But things that must get done, as well we know.

LOVE'S HARVEST

Love often starts with impulse, deep and warm,
Progressing to insatiable desire,
Then peaks and slowly mellows to a norm
That gently banks and regulates the fire.

So is it with each torrid love affair
That we of planet earth have ever known.
It's not that ardent lovers cease to care,
But just that in affection they have grown.

Love's passion lies concealed in embers deep
That yet retain their fervor and their glow.
Thus, as years go by, will lovers truly reap
Much more than they initially may sow.

Love's harvest does abundantly o'erflow,
When we allow our tenderness to grow.

OLD GLORY'S DIMENSIONS

On the Fourth of July, as I gazed at the flag,
That marvelous emblem of red, white and blue,
I was piqued by the scoundrels who think it a rag
And irked by how little it means to that few.

A rectangular swatch of motley design
Is all that myopic simpletons see,
Yet woven profoundly within its stout twine
Lie the seeds of our cherished liberty.

How can we with dispassion allow
Such deplorable nonsense undaunted to air?
Remember the sword that was made from a plow
And to battle how farmers bravely would dare?

Such disrespect all must staunchly assail
That our banner be tainted not with disdain,
That this hallowed experiment may ever prevail,
That sacrifice will not have been offered in vain.

Its stars and its stripes are symbols well known,
Reflecting our humble colonial birth
And the roots from which a proud people have grown
To fashion the greatest nation on earth.

But its colors are truly what stand it apart,
For they signify more than can ever be said.
Respect for inalienable rights they impart
And in them faith in the Lord can be read.

Its white stands for pure and virtuous thought
That inspired our Founders, fearless of death.
Its pallor envisions the span that was sought
In horizons of freedom with infinite breadth.

Blue is the sky, crowned by heaven above,
Where dwell lofty goals the lowest can reach,
And, pointing to God, it blends spirit and love
With values, which we to our children must teach.

Crimson's the blood that stains hallowed ground
And marks our concern for the human condition.
It's the pulsating strength with which we rebound
From disasters, which otherwise lead to perdition.

There's a little known fact that merits attention;
Old Glory indeed boasts a deep third dimension.

THE MARRIAGE DEBATE

There are issues on which government ought not opine
And it's for the courts to establish that line.
When it comes to marriage, the judges should state:
"You can't redefine what you didn't create!"

If injustice is found in existing law,
There are other ways to correct such a flaw.
The laws can be changed to clearly provide
That marital perks can elsewhere abide.

Marriage existed for eons before
Columbus and crew reached our eastern shore
And, designed as a heterosexual affair,
It's a religious sacrament that all Christians share.

If it's redefined, as progressives would like,
Religious intolerance surely will spike.
So, in mine fields let us not foolishly tread,
But let us simply adopt civil unions instead.

AUTHOR'S COMMENT: Don't throw the baby out with the bath water. My argument is that it was not necessary to redefine marriage. Same-sex relationships could be given official recognition as a form of civil union or a domestic partnership and legally accorded many of the benefits attributed to heterosexual marriage. If "equal protection" was really the objective (which I seriously doubt), it could have been accomplished without a direct attack on religion. I predict that the recent Supreme Court decision will result in a war against religion and will severely threaten the protections guaranteed by the establishment clause.

THE PARADOX OF LOVE

That love's a binding force no doubt is widely known,
Yet we fail to see the danger it imports,
For with affection's growth is disabling weakness sown,
As emotional defenses it contorts.

Although it's undisputed that love tightly binds us,
Yet it invariably exposes us to pain.
Only with our grievances forgiven and behind us
Can cherished relationships remain.

Ramparts we have built that loom above
By trust that flows from love are brought down low,
Whence comes the adage, "You hurt the ones you love,"
Which balladeers of old would often crow.

The paradox of love is, as it joins,
The armor of detachment it purloins.

MIRROR OF LOVE

A relationship concerning which I've smiled,
Because it's one I cannot comprehend,
Is that which binds a puppy to a child.
How can such opposing spirits blend?

Their greetings exude anticipation.
Each knows what the other has in mind.
There's no barrier. There's clear communication.
Such perfect unity is elsewhere hard to find.

Nature's rules have truly been suspended,
As if a beam was cast upon them from above,
As if what separates the species has now ended
And the puppy's but a mirror of his love.

A child and his dog are a pair to behold,
A relationship as rich as precious gold.

NORTHEND REVIEW

We were Hartford's brash northenders. 'Twas after World War II.
We thought that we were spiffy, but how little then we knew.
As we look back upon our day,
No remorse do we display,
For if we had to do it over, what we did is what we'd do.

Weaver High was the school that topped them all.
We were champs in academics and football.
There did discipline abound,
But we also screwed around,
And we chuckle when fond memories we recall.

Teachers then were concerned with more than pay,
And in their work put heart and soul every day.
There was no union to conceal
A teacher's lack of zeal,
And by law prayer in school was still okay.

Gretchen Harper was the one who taught us Latin.
She was tougher, it was said, than General Patton.
She seemed never to get tired
Of saying "Stand; you'll be inspired!"
'Twas the most demanding class we ever sat in.

Shuffling cards with a smirk out in the hall,
We never knew which one of us she'd call.
Your homework better be done.
We were always 'neath the gun;
She'd hide a quiz behind the map against the wall.

In teaching French, Miss Phillips took the prize,
Who, when she spoke or listened, closed her eyes.
We ne'er got through a class
Without a mention of Alsace,
Which to geography we later learned applies.

The foibles of our mentors we would tap,
Like Percy Owens, Porky Dow or Chalky Clapp.
A coin was flipped in study hall
To break the silence, I recall,
Causing veins in teacher's neck to bulge and snap.

At the blackboard, Mr. Clapp was in full view,
When his chin he'd rub with chalk, like a billiard cue,
And with Percy's velvet coat lapel,
And his affected speech, as well,
It's a wonder any knowledge e'er got through.

School buses in those days were not in style.
In groups we walked to school, more than a mile.
Brown bags we brought for lunch,
And when we bought, it wasn't much,
And now, when we look back, 'twas all worthwhile.

To religious use the auditorium was ceded,
When extra room by the synagogue was needed.
We thought that it made sense,
So no one took offense,
But today this by a lawsuit would be greeted.

Not everything was fun and you can bet
That tragedies occurred we can't forget;
That deadly circus fire
With its black smoke rising higher,
And how it filled us with such sadness and regret.

The diversity of our cultures was not news.
We were Wops and Micks and Pollocks, Blacks and Jews.
Yet, still we got along;
Our differences made us strong.
These are age-old lessons folks today should use.

Our sense of humor is what kept us all alive.
On ethnic jokes and corny digs we seemed to thrive.
Our respect for one another
Animosity would smother.
If we tried this stuff today, we'd not survive.

Whatever country from which our forebears came,
We held in deep respect our family name.
To fool around was fine,
But we had to toe the line,
Lest family honor we'd tarnish by our shame.

Our family life was prominent and strong.
We dared not do what parents thought was wrong.
A teacher's word was law,
Nor was there any flaw
In denying privileges that to us did not belong.

Teenage pregnancy was never something cool,
Nor did students ever bring a gun to school.
We knew wrong from what was right,
For our codes were black and white,
And never did today's confusion rule.

So profoundly did our peers and families care
That dropouts and teenage suicides were rare.
Drugs and liquor were taboo;
We had better things to do.
In those days we'd describe ourselves as "square."

Gay rights, bigotry and race discrimination
Were figments of a weird imagination.
We interacted; we had fun.
Each other's trust is what we won,
And this became the hallmark of our generation.

How we reacted with each other in those precious days gone by
Should be etched in solid stone and placed upon a mountain high
For all the world to read,
And hopefully to heed,
That the nonsense of today we may decry.

We had close to four hundred in our class,
And in intelligence most others we'd surpass.
About seventy percent
Of our group was college bent.
God, how did half a century ever pass?

So, let's say "Hail to Weaver High,
And the values we lived by."
Nothing I've said here is fiction,
So without fear of contradiction,
I declare that we were nifty,
For we're the Class of 1950!

AUTHOR'S COMMENT: This was a poem I wrote to celebrate my 50th high school reunion.

THE MESSAGE OF HIS LIFE

(A Eulogy To Frank Zuraski)

If e'er there lived a man of whom one could exclaim,
"My God! This person's everywhere, wherever there's a need,"
'Twas he, yes, Frank Zuraski was his name,
And the message of his life we all must heed.

Impatient in his zeal, he'd tackle every chore,
Kiwanis Club and Veterans' Post, a Newington parade,
From politics to civic groups, to monuments and more,
Such impact on our lives, no other's ever made.

The proof of his existence is everywhere we look.
His epitaph's the town we hold so dear.
Everything we cherish, every memory, every nook
Bears unmistakably his mark, indelible and clear.

His life can be reduced to a very simple phrase:
Love thy neighbor deeply, in a multitude of ways.

AUTHOR'S COMMENT: Frank Zuraski was a dear friend. He was
the epitome of brotherly love.

MOOSE ON THE LOOSE

We were frequently warned, as we toured in northern Maine,
That moose within our path were prone to wander,
And, as we leisurely proceeded along a rustic lane,
One suddenly appeared, causing me to ponder.

They're awkward looking critters, there's no avoiding that,
And I'm sure they're but minutely understood.
The bull wears an odd array of horns for a hat,
As aimlessly he wanders through the wood.

I wondered how they navigate through thickets, trees and brush
With those gawky, outspread antlers on their pate.
This leads me to believe that they're seldom in a rush,
Even on occasions when they're late.

I'm saddened by the cards, which by nature they've been dealt,
And to which this ballad sympathetically attests,
For though they're unattractive and preen no precious pelt,
Yet to hunt them from afar come hordes in orange vests.

I propose we turn the tables on those gun toting chaps
By providing those defenseless moose with bright orange caps.

PESKY DEMONS

That by demons we're possessed
Is for many not a joke.
They refuse to let us rest
And would bind us with a yoke.

Our forward progress they impede
And they hinder our repose.
Pretending to be what we need,
They hide beneath our very nose.

They distort and blur our vision
And reality assume.
They detour us from our mission
And would lead us to our doom.

Our demons we must neutralize
To alleviate the pain,
Yet in the meantime we must realize
That in us they'll remain.

When at last we recognize them,
It's clear that they've become a crutch.
It is then we must despise them
To escape their fatal clutch.

Yes, by demons we're possessed,
But we've the power to suppress them.
Be aware that they're a test,
Which we pass when we confess them.

Does the fact that demons haunt us
Mean we're hopelessly insane?
'Tis the query that will taunt us
And will answerless remain.

AUTHOR'S COMMENT: I hadn't seen a movie in quite a while and I had heard many favorable comments about "A Beautiful Mind." We decided to go out to dinner and see it for dessert. I was spiritually uplifted and deeply moved by this delectable, visual tiramisu. My emotions were drained and all I could think of was that this incredibly moving experience must be the essential goal cinematography was designed to attain. I couldn't wait to get home to memorialize my poetic interpretation of the message of this marvelous film.

I STOPPED TO SAY HELLO

Have you ever casually wandered down the street
And stopped to chat with someone you might know,
Then wondered, when the tirade was complete,
Why you ever chose to stop and say hello?

Exhausted, forlorn and aggravated,
You proceed to your appointed destination,
Bewildered by the fact that you'd been slated
To undergo such verbal indignation.

Frequently, I've suffered such assaults
And marveled at my patience and restraint.
Though I, like most, am plagued by petty faults,
Such episodes will make of me a saint.

Now, whenever I meander down the street,
I'm cautious about those whom I would greet.

WHAT'S MY LINE?

To instigate war between our cultures
Extremists will terrorize and kill.
With zeal they would feed us to the vultures,
As the blood of US citizens they'd spill.

They say that we are evil and Satanic,
Yet isn't that how we would picture them?
But it's they who create the fear and panic,
When on innocents they would rain mayhem.

This brings to mind a show called "What's My Line?"
Three subjects by a panel were deposed.
Two of them were phonies by design
And the celebrity was in the end exposed.

Stolid are their faces, as the trio sits and stares,
And now we hear a drum roll from the band.
When silenced is the rumble of the snares,
A voice says, "Will the real Satan stand?"

THE VIRTUE OF HYPOCRISY

To those who seek renown, I offer this advice:
"Values publicly expressed may incur substantial cost,
For the popular support one famous must entice
May through contentions of hypocrisy be lost."

Consider, if you will, this ironic set of facts:
Only those espousing virtue find themselves in peril's way.
He who lacks specific values is immune from all attacks,
While all others are condemned by what they say.

'Tis better to have statesmen proclaiming lofty goals,
Who at times succumb to weakness and may fall,
Than abdicate to leaders, who refuse to bare their souls,
Or who are guided not by principles at all.

Let occasional hypocrisy be fearlessly observed,
That values be proclaimed and thus preserved.

THE MOTHER OF SPILLS

The topic of the day is the environment's protection
And stringent regulations have been passed throughout the land.
Sites everywhere are suspect and subject to inspection
And mandates are applied very few can understand.

Governments spend millions, and so does every corporation,
To stop the toxic spills that cause our planet so much harm.
Environmental groups have been formed across the nation,
Perusing every power plant, factory and farm.

They complain about the Valdez and its arctic waters spill,
Of habitat destroyed, injured birds and tainted earth,
Of marine life, which in multitudes these foolish blunders kill,
And profoundly do we question progress and its worth.

We thus rely upon disclosures, heavy fines, the super lien,
As scientific testing precedes remediation.
In every type of industry threats of harm are seen
And producers are continually accused of rank evasion.

The cause, they lament, was the industrial revolution,
Which spawned manufacture and technology's advance.
But mythology discloses a more historic evolution,
Which in days of old occurred catastrophically by chance.

The world was first exposed to every kind of evil pox,
When haphazardly Pandora opened up her box.

AUTHOR'S COMMENT: See "Belated Blame" at p. 221.

THE PRICE OF SURVIVAL

'Twas autumn in the year two thousand one
With the World Series tied at three to three.
Before the final contest had begun,
Mariano piously addressed his coterie.

"The outcome is in the hands of God,"
Said the game's most respected closing ace.
In this context his remark did not seem odd,
Since apprehension could be seen on every face.

The Diamondbacks had clearly shown their stuff
And back at home were dauntless in their quest.
When the Yankees' mid-relievers had had enough,
It was time for them to call upon their best.

With the record for playoff and series saves,
There was little doubt that Moe could stem the tide,
But who could know how fickle luck behaves
And where elusive victory might reside?

Enrique Wilson was a teammate and Mariano's friend
And together they'd electrify their fans,
But none could now predict how this mystery game would end,
For its outcome was truly in God's hands.

Wilson had booked a homeward flight from New York City,
After the victory party that had been planned.
There they'd celebrate and their opponents pity,
Toasted heartily and greeted by a band.

In inning number nine, Rivera took the mound
And in humility allowed three runs to score.
Yankee fans were muted, making not a sound,
Mortally wounded to their very core.

Wilson scrapped his plans and took an early flight instead,
Burdened by the void of empty dreams.
Those on his original flight sadly turned up dead,
The victims of a fatal crash in Queens.

Had Mariano done what he was famous for,
Enrique, his friend, would be in the field no more.

AUTHOR'S COMMENT: The last game of the 2001 World Series is probably the most famous in baseball history. The New York Yankees were pitted against the Arizona Diamondbacks and the Series was tied at three to three. In a clubhouse team meeting prior to Game 7, Yankees closer, Mariano Rivera, who seldom commented at such meetings, closed the gathering with this statement, "Whatever happens tonight is in the hands of God." Enrique Wilson, a Yankee infielder, anticipating that his team would win the Series, booked a flight home to the Dominican Republic for November 12, 2001. The Series was delayed that year because of the September 11th attack. The flight selected by Wilson for his trip home allowed time for a parade in New York City and a celebration that would follow the final game. Game 7 was played on Sunday, November 4th in Phoenix, Arizona. With the Yankees leading in the bottom of the eighth inning, Joe Torre turned the game over to his ace closer, Mariano Rivera. Rivera struck out the side in the eighth, but in the bottom of the ninth, with the score tied and the bases loaded, Torre pulled the infield and outfield in to prevent the man on third from scoring. The Diamondbacks' Luis Gonzalez hit a bloop single over the drawn-in Derek Jeter and the man on third scored to give the Series to Arizona. As a result, Wilson booked an earlier flight home and American Airlines flight 587, which he had originally booked, crashed in Queens shortly after take-off, killing everyone on board. The following Spring Training, Rivera told Wilson that "I'm glad we lost the Series, because it means that I still have a friend."

LITTLE WHITE LIES

Whatever happened to the age-old art of selling,
To charming hucksters, who hawked their wares with skill?
The liberals, it seems, are now rebelling
In plaintiff tones, boisterous, sharp and shrill.

Whatever happened to the pitch-man, glib and tough,
Who peddled his products door to door?
With animation his baubles he would puff,
As the price of his merchandise would soar.

Whatever happened to sturdy self-reliance
And the law of sales we knew in years gone by?
Puffing is now met with staunch defiance
And harmless boasts we avidly decry.

A basic tenet of the common law of sales
Was that a vendor was allowed to puff his wares.
This doctrine today completely fails,
As our legal fabric suffers liberal tears.

Caveat emptor was the merchants' battle cry,
Which happily rid the courts of flimsy suits.
On custom in this age commerce dares not to rely,
For we've torn up our old familiar roots.

Truth inflexible has risen to the fore!
No leeway is accorded those who sell.
Hyperbole we tolerate no more,
As the rights of frail consumers now excel.

Those who fabricate the merchandise we buy
Find their promos sticking in their craw.
Though they may fabricate, they're not allowed to lie,
For this has now become the rigid law.

Yet, puffing by the plaintiffs was allowed,
When infamous tobacco suits were brought.
Should this turnabout make their lawyers proud
Of the legal contradiction that's been wrought?

Though they knew they were doing themselves harm,
When endlessly they puffed upon the weed,
Their assumption of the risk sounds no alarm,
As massive verdicts nourish liberal greed.

It was essential to adopt this point of view
That from defendants mighty verdicts would ensue.

AUTHOR'S COMMENT: When I was in law school, I took a course on the law of Sales. We learned about the common law doctrine that permitted vendors to "puff their wares." "Puffing" was considered a permissible art form and differentiated from misrepresentation. "Puffing" was defined as harmless exaggeration or hyperbole, "white lies," while "misrepresentation" was fraud. It was a matter of degree.

QUEST FOR ASYLUM

The Miami tribe of Elian Gonzalez
Are as crude as the Cuba that they fled.
Their desires must prevail "uber alles,"
As by hatred of Fidel they're blindly led.

On the one hand they demand their rights in law
And on the other that the law should be ignored.
Moved by wounds of separation that are raw,
They won't rest until their nemesis is gored.

Why do we confer on such narrow-minded groups
The power to such a conflagration now ignite,
Causing government to jump through flaming hoops
Without any recognition of what's right?

"If instead the claiming parent were a female,"
A commentator recently had joked,
"There's not the slightest doubt that she'd prevail,
For women's rights would have been invoked."

Or if the child were from a China or Iran,
It's absolutely clear what would be done.
We would disregard the culture where the episode began,
And reunite the parent with his son.

Although harm has been inflicted on this child
By all combatants in the ugly fray,
Greater still will be the injury compiled,
If the Miami family members get their way.

He survived imperiled straits.
He survived a stormy sea.
He survived his doomed shipmates,
But not his family.

AUTHOR'S COMMENT: This poem refers to the contentious situation that occurred in 2000, when Elian Gonzalez, a six year old Cuban boy, who had escaped from his homeland sought asylum in Florida. Without his father's knowledge, his mother attempted to escape from Cuba on a small boat with her son and boyfriend. When the boat capsized, his mother was drowned and Elian was rescued by two fishermen and turned over to the Coast Guard. He was later turned over to his paternal relatives in Miami. When his father demanded his return, his Miami relatives petitioned for asylum. Their petition was denied by a federal court. Miami-Dade County Mayor, Alex Penelas refused to allow his repatriation, until federal officials took him by force and returned him to Cuba.

REPARATIONS

Reparations have been sought by the present day descendants
Of those, who in days of yore did in bondage toil and sweat,
And successful corporations have been named as defendants
In suits claiming millions to repay what's claimed a debt.

I've pondered whether this should be allowed,
After so many fruitful years have passed.
Would winning such a cause make someone proud?
How long should such rights of action last?

The issue, of course, is complex and involved,
As discourse pro and con no doubt confirms.
Since the question remains completely unresolved,
To shed some light I'd pose it in these terms:

If reparations for slavery is the course we ought to choose,
Then how much should Egypt pay the Jews?

AUTHOR'S COMMENT: When the issue of reparations for slavery
came up, I became incensed. Slavery, of course, is a terrible
violation of human rights, but neither I nor my ancestors bear any
responsibility for that situation and we should not be burdened with
this form of retribution.

THE SAGA OF KIMBERLEY ROAD

'Twas the last day of May in seventy-eight.
The Council had met on that ominous date
To take up the question of Kimberley Road,
For tempers were high and about to explode.

"Whether to open a road that was closed?"
This was the query their petition had posed,
For the Cherry Hill group had persuaded Town Hall
That Kimberley Road was a path to the mall.

They claimed an invasion by out-of-town strangers,
Causing hazardous traffic and other such dangers.
Their children they feared this would disturb,
Forcing them back from both sidewalk and curb.

With a handful of votes politicians they bought
And the motion was passed, which they eagerly sought.
Then Kimberley Road, with blocks of concrete,
Was totally barred, but it wasn't their street.

Those directly affected took great offense,
For closing their street to them made no sense.
They got an injunction, but lost at the trial,
Unable to prove their position worthwhile.

The judge deeply feared that he was exposing
Children to danger and favored the closing.
As liberals are prone on occasion to do,
He'd yielded to emotional pleas from a few.

An event of great interest at this time took place,
During the stay for appeal of the case.
As soon as the Court had ruled for the Town,
The blocks of concrete again were put down.

When the losing party takes an appeal,
The law imposes a stay that is real.
The status quo must thus be observed,
Until the decision is held undisturbed.

The Court found the Council to be in contempt
And ordered a fine for this futile attempt.
The road again open, when the blocks were withdrawn,
Continued ill-feelings to nurture and spawn.

A petition was filed and a plebiscite held.
The answer was clear, but the storm was not quelled.
The count favored opening about ten votes to one,
But despite this result, a new suit was begun.

In the meantime the folks in the neighboring Town
Truckloads of earth on the road had thrown down.
This they then graded and spread with grass seed
And made claim of a title by way of a deed.

From the builder they claimed this land to receive,
Attempting the public to fool and deceive.
But the Town's right-of-way encumbered the fee
And who owned beneath mattered not legally.

To date this poor road comes abrupt to an end,
Turning neighbor on neighbor and friend against friend.
It stands as a warning to the leaders of towns
That, where pettiness lurks, poor judgment abounds.

The Kimberley question in this manner evolved
And God only knows if it will ever be solved.

AUTHOR'S COMMENT: Kimberly Road is a short street located in the northwest corner of Newington, a short distance from the Westfarms Mall. The street is in a residential subdivision and runs in a northerly direction to the West Hartford line. In 1978 it continued under a different name into West Hartford, leading to other roads which provided access to the mall. When the mall was constructed, residents in the adjacent Cherry Hill area feared that Kimberley Road would be used as a shortcut to the mall, creating traffic problems in this residential area. The residents on nearby Cherry Hill Drive petitioned the Newington Town Council to close Kimberley Road at the town line. The Town Council granted their petition and closed the road, using large concrete barriers. The residents living on Kimberley Road wanted their street to remain open and retained my office to take legal action to reopen their street. On their behalf, I brought suit for a mandatory injunction requiring the Town to remove the barriers and reopen the road. A preliminary injunction was granted and the barriers were removed. When the case was tried, the Court ruled in favor of the Town. I immediately filed an appeal, which automatically requires maintenance of the status quo. Disregarding the stay, the Town quickly replaced the barriers. I then filed a Motion for Contempt of Court and the Town was again ordered to remove the barriers under penalty of a substantial fine. Before the matter could be resolved legally, the Town of West Hartford removed their portion of the road and the legal issues in Newington became moot.

Photo by E. G. Pizzella

P. J. TOPCAT

DEDICATED TO DEAR FRIENDS
WHO NEARLY LOST THEIR CHERISHED PET

P. J. Topcat, where the devil have you gone?
Said he: "I chased a bumble bee,
And scampered on the lawn."

P.J. Topcat, where'd you go from there?
"I climbed a weeping willow,
And dangled in mid air."

P.J. Topcat, how got you up so high?
"When I beheld that vicious dog,
I thought that I could fly."

P.J. Topcat, we combed the neighborhood!
"I know you did. I saw you,
As in that tree I stood."

P.J. Topcat, we feared the very worst!
"Well, so did I, as up so high,
That wicked cur I cursed."

P.J. Topcat, why'd you stay away so long?
"I meowed all day and meowed all night,
But no one heard my song."

P.J. Topcat, what lesson did you learn?
"Whene'er I see a canine,
Homeward I'll return."

P.J. Topcat, are you happy to be home?
"You bet your life and here I'll stay,
Never more to roam."

P.J. Topcat, you gave us quite a scare!
"I know I did, but bear in mind
We cats have lives to spare."

BITTEN BY THE BUG

Oh child of mine!
Why waste you time in frivolous pursuits,
As stubbornly you practice and rehearse?
You persevere, yet meager are the fruits
And it costs you some to make the matter worse.

Oh mother dear!
I know you deeply care and love me so
And surely from concern your words must come,
But the fire within my breast you'll never know,
Nor how I to this endeavor did succumb.

Oh child of mine!
Come on! Get real! Give up your dream of fame.
Come back to earth and spend some time with us.
Beyond this place none recognize your name,
So why persist and why make so much fuss?

Oh mother dear!
I effervesce and thrill so on the stage.
I soar to heights I'd nowhere else attain.
There I test my limits, from joy to utter rage.
I'm energized, triumphant, proud and vain.

Oh child of mine!
Tend you your business and your cluttered space.
Leave acting to those without a life.
Seek the comfort of friends and home with grace.
Avoid the actor's guilt and inner strife.

Oh mother dear!
On stage "I've slipped the surly bonds of earth
And danced the skies on laughter-silvered wings."
No feat to me so proves that I have worth,
As when I don the garb of feckless fools and kings.

Oh child of mine!
Do you really think they know how hard you work
And all you sacrifice to furnish their diversion?
Those whom you neglect will say you shirk,
That your theatrical involvement's mere perversion.

Oh mother dear!
The art is in my soul. I can't resist.
Such power's bliss, to make them laugh and cry.
And when I can't be there, to know that I am missed.
Stay home and watch TV? I'd rather die!

AUTHOR'S COMMENT: The quote about slipping the surly bonds of earth and dancing the skies on laughter-silvered wings is taken from one of my favorite poems, "High Flight" by John Gillespie Magee, Jr. I memorized and passionately recited this poem in my eighth grade English class at Northeast Junior High School in Hartford and it was there that I acquired my intense interest in poetry.

Photo by S. J. Miller

THE CAPTAIN ON THE BRIDGE

Welcoming the billows and ripples on the tide,
With sextant and compass and glowing stars above,
His eager craft upon the main he pilots far and wide
And demonstrates the measure of his love.

Standing stalwart at the helm, undeterred by rolling haze,
The wheel clenched firmly in his grip,
Resolute and focused is his perceptive gaze,
As he deftly charts his course and guides his ship.

Ignoring the foibles and frivolities of man,
Relentless and steadfast in his determination,
He guards the approach to that serpentine span
That joins Prince Edward Island to his nation.

Unaffected by trite and superficial notion,
The Captain on the Bridge shows his devotion.

AUTHOR'S COMMENT: The above photo was taken on our trip to Nova Scotia. I was impressed by this solemn and overpowering statue at the foot of the bridge connecting Prince Edward Isle to the mainland.

Printed in the United States
By Bookmasters